Women and Spirituality

New Feminist Perspectives Series
General Editor: Rosemarie Tong, Davidson College

Claiming Reality: Phenomenology and Women's Experience
by Louise Levesque-Lopman

Evidence on Her Own Behalf: Women's Narrative as Theological Voice
by Elizabeth Say

Feminist Jurisprudence: The Difference Debate
edited by Leslie Friedman Goldstein

Is Women's Philosophy Possible?
by Nancy J. Holland

Manhood and Politics: A Feminist Reading of Political Theory
by Wendy L. Brown

"Nagging" Questions: Feminist Ethics in Everyday Life
edited by Dana E. Bushnell

Rethinking Ethics in the Midst of Violence: A Feminist Approach to Freedom
by Linda A. Bell

Speaking from the Heart: A Feminist Perspective on Ethics
by Rita C. Manning

Take Back the Light: A Feminist Reclamation of Spirituality and Religion
by Sheila Ruth

Toward a Feminist Epistemology
by Jane Duran

Voluptuous Yearnings: A Feminist Theory of the Obscene
by Mary Caputi

Women, Militarism, and War: Essays in History, Politics, and Social Theory
edited by Jean Bethke Elshtain and Sheila Tobias

Women, Sex, and the Law
by Rosemarie Tong

Women and Spirituality, Second Edition
by Carol Ochs

Women and Spirituality

Second Edition

Carol Ochs

ROWMAN & LITTLEFIELD PUBLISHERS, INC.
Lanham · Boulder · New York · London

ROWMAN & LITTLEFIELD PUBLISHERS, INC.

Published in the United States of America
by Rowman & Littlefield Publishers, Inc.
4720 Boston Way, Lanham, Maryland 20706

3 Henrietta Street
London, WC2E 8LU, England

British Cataloging in Publication Information Available

Library of Congress Cataloging-in-Publication Data

Ochs, Carol.
    Women and spirituality / Carol Ochs. —2nd ed.
        p.   cm. — (New feminist perspectives series)
    Includes bibliographical references and index.
    1. Women—Religious life.   2. Women and religion.
    3. Women in the Bible.   I. Title. II. Series.
  BL625.7.O24   1996
  291.4'082—dc20   96-29291
                                             CIP

ISBN 0–8476–8329–X (cloth : alk. paper)
ISBN 0–8476–8330–3 (pbk. : alk. paper)

Printed in the United States of America

™ The paper used in this publication meets the minimum requirements of
American National Standard for Information Sciences—Permanence of
Paper for Printed Library Materials, ANSI Z39.48–1984.

To

Elisabeth Amy,
Miriam Adina,
and Cheryl Lea

Contents

Introduction		ix
Acknowledgments		xi
Prologue		1
1	Ecstasy, Religion, and Spirituality	5
2	The Context of Spirituality	15
3	Women and Spirituality	27
4	A Spirituality of This World	45
5	Circumstance, Conflict, Suffering, and Guilt	57
6	Death	71
7	Love, Unity, Joy, Contribution, and Birth	89
8	Beyond Solitude to Compassion	103
9	The Spiritual Walk	113
10	Time	129
11	A New Spirituality	145
Notes		159
Works Cited		167
Index		173
About the Author		179

Introduction

Fourteen years have passed since the first appearance of *Women and Spirituality*. The obvious changes in the world and the personal changes in my own life have led me to reflect on the meaning of time. Time plays a central role in the Western religious traditions because both Judaism and Christianity are historical religions—that is, revelation takes place in time, and the passage of events in time informs us about the nature of reality. That shouldn't be surprising: If the events of our lives don't instruct us, why are we living?

Time, or events in time, initially led to my writing *Women and Spirituality*. I had moved from young womanhood to motherhood and the implications of that transformation changed my way of being in the world. Now, at this new time of life, I am still a mother, but that role has radically changed. No longer do I get up nights to care for my daughters. These children are now independent women, living productive lives in other cities. The love that motherhood created has not changed, but its forms of expression have altered irrevocably. This second edition of the book offers a new chapter that explores women's unique relationship to time and how that relationship helps us understand this central category and aids us all in our spiritual quest. In the first edition I offered two positive role models for women: Hagar, whose role as woman of the desert is in stark contrast with the Desert Fathers of early Christianity, and Leah, who exemplifies the heroism of resiliency. I have added two additional role models in the course of this new edition: Elisheba, wife of Aaron and mother of Nadab and Abihu, who offers an example of authentic mourning, and Miriam, the prophet, whose story exemplifies the new spirituality. Briefer additions sprinkled throughout the book are aimed at bringing the ideas into sharper focus.

Women once again have begun to claim their authentic voices and live out their ways of relating to God. At first, only the women themselves were affected, but increasingly the results can be found as well in their religious institutions. In the past generation, women have begun to attend seminaries in significant numbers, often without knowing whether or not they would be allowed to receive ordination. Among Jews, women rabbis did not become a reality until 1972, and although eleven women were ordained as Episcopal priests in 1974, the corporate church did not authorize such ordinations until 1977. Those original female clergy made a profound contribution in their lonely pioneering stance. Still, they had only male clergy to use as models. It took the passage of time before women ceased being female versions of male ministers, priests, or rabbis. They had had different experiences from those of men and could bring different insights to their congregations.

Indeed, women's perspective has found its way into institutional religion—a major change since this book first appeared. As women increasingly bring their own values and perspectives into leadership roles, we can expect more and greater transformations. The house of worship will become a *home* of worship, a place where major human concerns are addressed. The emphasis will shift from external texts to internal, personal ones. People will change their relationship to time. Male clergy have traditionally taken on several roles: as keepers of the gate, determining who will and will not enter; as holy people, serving as models for their congregations; and even as judges. Clergywomen see their vocation as hosts welcoming everyone into the home of God. (A good host is sensitive to the different needs of every guest and strives to make the visit a fulfilling one.)

These are only some of the changes brought about by women's greater participation in the formal religious sphere. It is hoped that this revised and enlarged edition of *Women and Spirituality* will help more women contribute their special insights to the spiritual life of humanity in the twenty-first century.

Acknowledgments

I am grateful to Sheila Ruth for her insightful suggestions for improving the book, to Jennifer Ruark for her support in bringing this new edition to press, and Michael Ochs, not merely for providing encouragement, insights, and editorial skills, but, above all, for sharing his life with mine.

Prologue

When I completed my first book, *Behind the Sex of God,* I knew I had set myself a religious agenda, but I was not clear how it would unfold. Its progression has been at times surprising to me, although in retrospect it seems both obvious and logical. In that book I had been concerned with the ways in which we think about religion in patriarchal and matriarchal systems. I then studied the role of ecstasy in the philosophical systems of Plato, Spinoza, Shaftesbury, Kant, and Freud. I did not realize at the time that I wanted to go beyond conceptual systems to the actual experiences that underlay them. Then I changed pace completely to write a novel (unpublished) that also reflects my religious agenda, exploring the conflicting demands of the protagonist's covenant with God and with his wife and unborn child.

A question that arose as a result of my first book had finally found expression. I did not want to know how to talk about God. I wanted to know how to live—and how my experiences shaped the answer to that question. In the quest for an answer, I sought to go beyond ethics to religion, which I regard to be the grounding of ethics. But I knew that religion could not be simply a name for a social institution; it had to point to something of deeper and more enduring value. I found the definition that gave expression to my inchoate notion in John Dunne's *The Way of All the Earth:* "Religion is insight into the common experiences of mankind." I also discovered how seldom religion took into account the experiences of women. As I focused more narrowly on those people whose lives were centered on religion—the great authors of the Western spiritual tradition—I was appalled to find no text written from the viewpoint of a woman who was both a mother and happily married. I searched further, convinced that I had overlooked an obvious classic. I failed to come up with any examples in writings on religion, spirituality, or philosophy. (While some can be found in the form of fiction, diaries, and autobiography, these do not deal explicitly with spirituality.) I began to wonder what would have happened had there been such a book. How much of what I believe about reality—about the value of life and its meaning—is the result of having lived in marriage for nearly twenty-five years and having raised two daughters to adulthood? Had the "saints" raised an infant to adulthood, would they still have come up with the "purgative way"?

If religion is insight into experience, a religion developed out of partial experience cannot be adequate to the needs of a full humanity. I felt a great need to complete the vision offered by some of the great spiritual teachers not because I have deeper insights, but because as a woman, as a person living in union and communion with another, as a mother, and as a person living outside an intentional religious community, I have had different experiences on which to reflect.

The great spiritual figures have traditionally been understood to develop along the same lines as other people, but to have developed further. Since traditional spirituality has been male-centered, it has been regarded as an extension of the male maturational process that emphasizes individuation—coming into selfhood. The new spirituality offered here is an extension of the female maturational process that emphasizes nurturing—coming into relationship.

This book is not autobiographical, and I do not chart the many false turns I have taken before getting down to the business of simply trusting my own experience. I attempt to show how women *as* women can contribute uniquely to our understanding of spirituality. In trying to prod people to pay attention to their own experiences, I employ two biblical role models, Hagar and Leah, and explore mothering as a context for spirituality. Growing out of our experiences of having been mothered (an experience we recover in the process of mothering) is a need to examine and reject "otherworldliness." A closer look at traditional "otherworldly" claims suggests that we may be misinterpreting what the mystics are really trying to tell us: that our world is not wrong, but our way of relating to it is.

The "otherworldly" claim retains its attractiveness not because of the mystics' utterances, but because this world is frequently a harsh and painful one. I examine those difficult conditions that cause us to long for an escape: circumstance, conflict, guilt, suffering, and death. I add experiences that equally comprise a part of the human condition, but that traditional writers on spirituality, expressing only a male-centered point of view, have chosen to neglect: love, accord, joy, and birth.

Mystics have usually been pictured as struggling alone for their salvation. Women who are aware of the dependency of infancy and the mutuality of marriage can show that the spiritual struggle is shared and that salvation is the overcoming of separation. Finally, women can raise questions about the prevalent metaphor of the spiritual life as a "journey," with its implicit notion of linear progression and "stages."

After expanding or complementing traditional spirituality with the perspectives brought by women, I formulate those insights at which women can arrive by reflection on their own experience, independent of any comparative or complementary structure. This represents the "new spirituality" that includes women's contribution to a spirituality adequate to humanity's needs.

The experience of mothers and other women transforms the traditional notion of spirituality. But the new spirituality described here is only *formulated* through the insights growing out of these experiences. Its *practice,* as a way of life, is not restricted to mothers, or even to women alone.

The reader will note that I refer throughout the book to "mother" and "mothering," although I am aware that in all but a few instances, the neutral terms "parent" and "parenting" might at first glance have been preferable. But to "de-feminize" the book in that way would have compromised two of my major points: (a) that women, in whatever roles they have chosen or—more usually—been thrust, can contribute in a unique way to the attainment of spirituality by *all;* and (b) that the mothering process itself (in which male participation has been virtually non-existent for millennia) provides an unusually good context for spirituality. At the same time it is my fervent hope that, instead of endorsing a particular role in life for women, I succeed in opening everyone to new, more natural possibilities for spirituality.

In the process of trying to expand the traditional views of spirituality, I have had the joyous experience of "discovering" many books. An extensive list appears in the bibliography, but a few landmarks deserve mention here. Of the books about mysticism, the most useful for my study has been Evelyn Underhill's classic, *Mysticism.* Of the works by mystics, I have found Meister Eckhart's the most rewarding. The psychological perspective that has most influenced my thinking is that of D. W. Winnicott. The theologians whose works have deeply affected me are Martin Buber and John S. Dunne. And the philosopher whose vision continues to guide my own is Baruch Spinoza.

Chapter 1

Ecstasy, Religion, and Spirituality

The basic terms we use in thinking about spirituality are not value-free. The way we define ecstasy, religion, and spirituality already reveals our basic commitment—whether that definition embraces the fullness of the human experience, which a feminist view would have to do, or whether it has the bias of a traditional male-centered spirituality. The capacity for abstract reason has, for the long history of Western thought, been ascribed to men, while women have been thought to be emotional, that is, irrational. We need to recognize that to be human is to be capable of both reason and emotional engagement.

Traditional spirituality has been suspicious of experience and favored instead the role of reason. To complement this notion we will begin with a discussion of an experiential concept—ecstasy—on the grounds that reason *alone* is not adequate to realize our full humanity and that we need our full humanity to achieve spirituality.

Implicit in feminist spirituality is the view that experience must have a privileged place. This is true as well for theology and epistemology (ways of knowing), two components of spirituality. Experience is primary because each of our lives is as significant and serious as any life that has ever been lived on this planet. In other words, no one was created as a bit player for someone else's drama. Each life is sacred, and in each life we can find the entire cosmic drama, from creation to revelation to redemption. Thus, authority and tradition do not have pride of place (although we learn from both). Instead, we let our own lives serve as sacred texts to be studied and valued.

ECSTASY

"The greatest blessings come by way of madness, indeed of madness that is heaven-sent." The poet is "stimulated to rapt passionate expression" by this madness; the prophet attests "to the superiority of heaven-sent madness over man-made sanity"; and the lover is bequeathed "a sort of madness [that] is the gift of the gods, fraught with the highest bliss." So begins Plato's defense of love in his dialogue the *Phaedrus*.[1] Plato is not lauding the artistry of a particular poet or praising the insight of one certain oracle; he is describing aspects of the human condition, potentialities that lie within us all.

We have all been touched by the kind of divine madness that Plato describes. Some shrink from its touch and bury the experience in the dark recesses of their memory. Others celebrate the experience as a gift of ecstasy and use it as the touchstone of reality. They construct magnificent religious systems rooted in their experiences of ecstasy, systems sustained and nourished through this rooting. Theologians, traditionally wary of experience, are perhaps most wary of the ecstatic experience. Yet at the root of their theology is an experience that was once deeply felt by their predecessors.

Some who experience ecstasy dismiss the feeling as an aberration, as adolescent fervor, or as the result of too much intoxicating drink. Others, including many twentieth-century philosophers, theologians, and literati, may accept the importance of emotion but focus on despair, or anguish, or fear, and don't take these feelings to the point of ecstasy. Ecstasy, as it will be used throughout this book, is the standing outside of oneself *(ex stasis)*. This means that the normal self, which includes our usual ways of thinking, judging, and evaluating, is displaced. We are brought outside the self through an irruption in our life. While ecstasy is usually accompanied by a strong feeling, such as extreme joy or extreme grief, its essential characteristic is the displacement of our usual sense of who we are and how we think. "Ecstasy implies a passing beyond all the conceptual thinking of the discursive reason."[2] Whether ecstasy is brought on by grief, suffering, joy, or love, it is an experience equally authentic and significant for coming to understand reality and our relationship to it. Plato focuses on an expansive kind of love.[3] Contemporary writers on death, such as Elisabeth Kübler-Ross and Robert J. Lifton, also deal with love, but their primary concern is with the working through of grief and mourning to discover a love that can live through death. (Suffering and death will be discussed more fully in later chapters.)

How does an ecstatic experience actually feel? Surely all of us have had such an experience, yet we cannot express it; we can only point to some characteristics and hope to evoke memories of it. Life is made up of ordinary objects and repetitive events that fill time and space. Then, unexpectedly, the ordinary becomes the vessel of the extraordinary. The feeling can be described as an awareness of otherness that is beyond our ability to control. It is a force pitted against us, a force that is alive and that imbues our own life with meaning. The force may come through a powerful work of art that grips us, a religious feeling that invades us, or a love experience that electrifies our world. The feeling may come in the sudden anticipation of a loss or at the moment when a loss is fully grasped; it may come during conflict or when accepting responsibility; it may come at the birth of a child. Initially, then, the cause for ecstasy is the anomalous or the unexpected. As we grow more open to reality, more willing to hold in abeyance our normal concepts of thinking and judging, the ecstatic experience comes more frequently, and the causes are less and less extraordinary. J. H. Jowett makes this point in the form of a prayer:

O Lord, keep me sensitive to the grace that is round about me. May the familiar not become neglected! May I see Thy goodness in my daily bread, and may the comfort of my home take my thoughts to the mercy seat of God![4]

Ernest Becker emphasizes the same idea:

The great boon of repression is that it makes it possible to live decisively in an overwhelmingly miraculous and incomprehensible world, a world so full of beauty, majesty, and terror that if animals perceived it all they would be paralyzed to act.[5]

Ernst Cassirer has suggested that the experience of what we call ecstasy is so significant that we want to do something with it. So we create a *mythos* to make sense of it and supply a name that enables us to hold it in memory and recall it for further examination. The name and myth may eventually become reified into a rational system, but always behind this rational structure is the experience of ecstasy that bodied it forth.[6] Should we stray too far from the original felt experience, we will lose the life force and will be dealing with a dead system that cannot finally touch our lives.

Society, meanwhile, considers the experience of ecstasy to be dangerous—the experience of the mad. It frightens us, for example, that the same Psalmist who can glory that one should "taste and see that the Lord is good" can at other times, when the feeling of ecstasy is not present, experience the most profound despair. This awareness of danger results in society's trying to tame and control the experience by creating safe outlets for it and situations in which it can occur, such as institutionalized religious practices and institutionalized social mores of personal interaction. But all attempts to control and tame what is essentially uncontrollable and seemingly possessed of a life of its own carry a twofold risk of (a) controlling something other than what was intended and (b), perhaps more dangerous, deadening the source of life. And yet the fear of ecstasy is legitimate. The quest for this emotion can lead to a frightening narcissism. When people seek ecstasy in sex or drugs, they can become blinded to the needs of others. Slowly, we learn not to seek ecstasy but to discover it in dailiness.

Ecstasy is real, and it signals a radical shift in our way of understanding and perceiving reality. If we give ourselves permission to use the language of normative religion when speaking of the ecstatic experience, then we can suddenly recognize revelation in the context of our own lives. When used in the Western religious tradition, the term "revelation" conjures up the giving of the law at Mount Sinai. But when people are asked to speak of revelation in their own lives— applying that majestic term to their experiences—they discover one experience after another that fits the term. Soon they begin to recognize ongoing revelation in the course of their days. Sometimes the revelation has specific content: *this is the road you should take.* Sometimes the content is more like: *I am with you.* One mother reported that as she lay awake after her first child's birth, she didn't think how beautiful the baby was or how much it resembled her husband; rather, she thought, "I am a partner in Creation."

RELIGION

Ideally, after having undergone an ecstatic experience—standing outside our self—we reflect back on this experience and communicate it. All too often, we are led to undervalue our experience and even be dismissive of it. But if we are encouraged to value it and integrate it into our lives, we discover that it carries a moral imperative. In time, this reflection and communication can become a comprehensive vision of reality. The result of such working through of insights occasioned by one or more extraordinary experiences is a religious system. Once we recognize that the extraordinary experience includes, for example, love, joy, fear, guilt, loss, birth, and death, we realize that the extraordinary experience is common to all people. Commenting on this idea, John Dunne notes that "the experiences on which the religions were based were common experiences, and that the uncommon thing was the insight into the experiences."[7] From the realization that common experiences form the basis of religion, we arrive at a definition of religion as "insight into the common experiences of humankind."[8] By focusing on our common experiences, religion emphasizes the meaningfulness of what we do and experience on earth. "The mighty revelations to which the religions appeal are like in being with the quiet revelations that are to be found everywhere and at all times."[9] It follows, then, that what happens to us here is important, valuable, and revealing of the nature of reality and of how we ought to live. But we must understand that merely having experiences guarantees nothing. Religion in its true sense emphasizes the insight into our experiences and the consciousness that insists on learning something from them.

Buddha's enlightenment can be viewed in this context. It begins with his seeing an old person, a sick person, and a corpse. These experiences are not unusual; many of us have shared them, although few have achieved enlightenment through them. Buddha's religious enlightenment comes about only when he tries to understand what the experiences mean and what he can learn from them about the nature of human life.

Building religion on insight into experience does not mean choosing one set of experiences as normative. It suggests that all of our experiences are subject to reflection and exploration. And the goal of this reflection is not another experience but a relationship. Relationships are made up of experiences, of keeping promises, of knowing, and of nurturing.

Defining religion as insight into the common experiences of humankind reveals our feminist perspective both by what it leaves out and by what it emphasizes. Our definition is silent about structures, doctrines, and hierarchies. It focuses on something that is available to all people equally—their own experience. In reemphasizing the value and significance of our world, this definition carries forth women's central insight.

SPIRITUALITY

If religion is insight into our experiences, it must result from thinking about what our senses and emotions tell us. The process is largely cognitive—that is, a matter of thinking—although not exclusively so, since thinking about our experiences imbues them with meaning and transforms them. Still, religion is primarily a conceptual system. We have need, however, for something that can take us beyond cognition. We experience, and we reflect on our experiences, but more than that, we have a relationship to our experiences and reflections. The active, conscious, and deliberate process of coming into this relationship is the beginning of spirituality.

Having such a relationship means living, and reflecting on our living. It means accepting or rejecting, consenting or denying, loving or enduring one's life. We realize that our relationship to life is of a different order from life itself and has the power to affect the nature of our experiences. Moreover, meaning and value reside not in life, which is merely lived, but in our relationship to life.

Our experiences, our reflection on our experiences, and our relation to these experiences create a gateway to reality. When our perception of an event differs from that of other people, we become aware that reality is something larger than our experience of it. Instead of judging that others misperceive the event, we feel compassion for them—that is, we see it from their perspective. This perspective expands our own reality. Reality, then, is that which is larger than our experiences and our consciousness. It enables our consciousness to grow, expand, and be transformed.

This process of coming into relationship with reality is spirituality. In defining spirituality as a process, we must understand an active and conscious participation in reality. The process entails motion, change, and growth—a transformation of our being and consciousness. The definition also includes relationship. This implies an awareness that spirituality is not merely a way of knowing, but also a way of being and doing: "All real living is meeting."[10] Thus, our definition affirms that we are in process, or change, in order to meet, confront, and truly connect with that which is real.

In an essential way, the spiritual person must walk alone. If the great spiritual teachers were like the great founders of scientific revolutions, then when one of them "got it right," we would have the basis for a new paradigm and could build from there. But the spiritual person who is searching for the God within is seeking something unique, and no spiritual teacher can offer an answer. Rather, the teacher can model for us a process that each of us must undergo in order to achieve our authentic self. The spiritual person is not one who says, in effect, "let me do it for you," but one who says, "this is how to do it." We cannot inherit anyone's relationship to God. Rather, we can inherit the realization that our own relationship to God is what counts, and that the relationship must be individually arrived at through be-ing open, responsive, and authentic.

Many definitions of traditional spirituality include turning away from this world and recognizing the transcendent. The term "transcendent" was originally used in a dualistic sense: it referred to spirit as op-posed to matter, the other world as opposed to this world. Feminist spirituality has made us aware of this dualism and led us to challenge it. Spirituality encompasses all of our being: mind *and* heart, strength *and* energy. Spirituality aims at transforming this world so that it more nearly resembles the ideal other world that is our model.

Definitions of traditional spirituality grow out of the view that spir-ituality is the highest state of maturity. When maturity is seen in terms of a male developmental model, our highest task is to achieve indi-viduation. This requires separation of the self from its supporting en-vironment. The female developmental model focuses on relationship. Women's contribution to spirituality—the insight of their intercon-nectedness—is that full human maturity must entail coming into rela-tionship with reality.

ROLE OF EXPERIENCE IN SPIRITUALITY

Our definition of spirituality as the process of coming into relation-ship with reality grows out of—and must continually be tested against—our actual experience of living in this world. If we experi-ence ecstasy when we watch our infant go from frenzied crying to falling asleep peacefully in our arms, then that experience is real and significant, and any account of reality will have to be consistent with that data. We must not, however, allow the experience to become an end in itself. Twentieth-century psychology has taught us to focus on our emotional experiences, or feelings. They are to the mental life what sensory experience, or perception, is to the physical life. Although people will disagree on precise definitions of feelings, the feelings can nevertheless be identified and named. But just as sensory experience can become science only by being thought about and understood as the external manifestation of an underlying theory or law, so emotional experiences contribute to our spirituality only by being similarly understood as components of the life that gives rise to them. In short, experience, being part of life, cannot be the goal of the spiritual life.

Despite the argument that experience is not the goal of the spir-itual life, much writing on spirituality has confused the means with the end. In spirituality we find a conscious, deliberate transformation of the self to bring it into closer relationship with reality. The transformation requires many steps, some of which may be accompanied by intensely felt experiences. Too often, people examining the spiritual life focus on these experiences—the ecstasies, raptures, or paranormal events—and on methods for achieving them. But an experience is merely an event in one's life. It can become meaningful only by reflection and incorporation into a system built on insight into human experience. If the essential component of spirituality, the transformation of the self, is deemphasized or ignored, then the spiritual quest is sidetracked. "So we should not embark on the ascetic life in the hope of seeing visions clothed with form or shape; for if we do, Satan will find it easy to lead our soul astray."[11] This passage warns us that we should not take lights, visions, auditions, or even visitations from angels too seriously; what is important is the life of works and prayer; anything that distracts one from this spiritual practice is suspect.

Other dangers are inherent in focusing on experience as an end in itself. In their quest, mystics often ignore the more usual in favor of the unaccustomed, transcendental, paranormal experiences. Inevitably, this focus leads to a devaluing of much of what we do and experience on earth, the everyday and commonplace, in favor of those few moments of extreme sensation. Rather than trying to find insight in all that occurs, we are tempted to seek those rarefied experiences. "But the central reality of the everyday hour on earth, with a streak of sun on a maple twig and the glimpse of the eternal *Thou,* is greater for us than all enigmatic webs on the brink of being."[12]

Another problem occasioned by a focus on experience alone lies in the resulting tendency toward self-centeredness, which is opposed to the insight at the heart of the deepest spirituality. It fosters self-gratification ("I want to have this experience") and competitiveness ("My ecstasy outlasted yours"), a fearful focusing on the self that is exactly counter to the standing outside the self of genuine ecstasy. A related problem is brought about when experiences of different people are compared to one another. Comparison leads to classification and ranking—these experiences are good, these are better, those are bad. We learn from all our experiences. Pain is a genuine and significant signal, although we may prefer pleasure. If we take anger, boredom, depression, or fear to signal a "fall from grace," we may be unwilling to recognize them when they occur. We cannot benefit from our experiences unless we can truly feel them and claim them for ourselves. But if our experience, which should put us in touch with what is most truly ours, is measured against external standards, it can actually foster inauthenticity.

Finally, focusing on emotional experiences alone might lead us to confuse the experience with the reality that underlies it. For example, love has sometimes been identified with a feeling, or constellation of feelings, rather than with the life of which it is a part. Love, as we will see later, is neither sentimentality nor fleeting sensations. It is a way of devotion, physical caring, and emotional concern. Just as the spirituality of the Desert Fathers lay in their work and prayer and not in the accompanying lights and visions, so genuine love lies in its practice, daily devotions, and ministrations—not in the accompanying racing heart or ecstatic experience.

Once we realize that experience is not a goal, we must reaffirm its importance as a means when we learn to trust ourselves and to be true to ourselves. Religion and spirituality do not spring up as answers to abstract questions—they are our responses to what we experience. They must be true to our experience or else they do not accord with their fundamental purpose. If religion is to be insight into *all* human experience, then it must speak about—and to—our *individual* experience. If spirituality is the process of coming into relationship with reality, then it must include a relationship with the reality of our own experiences.

We should not seek experiences but should pay attention to those we have. We should not cultivate ecstasies but should remain open to the lessons they offer us. In short, we should live our lives in an awake, aware fashion, honestly claiming for ourselves what belongs to us: our joy, our pain, our generous impulses, our anger. By authentically claiming our experiences, we can begin to come into relationship with them and, through this process, travel further on our path to spirituality.

Chapter 2

The Context of Spirituality

Once we acknowledge the rightful place of experience in spirituality, something both obvious and startling becomes apparent. The spiritual life is not forced, contorted, agonized, or rare—it is ordinary, readily available, and it surrounds us all. We are not seeking ecstasies, but are open to the ecstasies around us. We are not seeking visions, auditions, trances, or the gift of tongues, but insight into the joy, despair, loss, trust, and transformations that comprise human life. Life is so structured that we may all reflect on the inherent ecstasies and come into relationship with reality.

NATURALNESS OF THE SPIRITUAL LIFE

At any point in our lives, we are letting go of earlier images of our selves and the lives that went with them, and gaining new experiences and potential insight. We are always undergoing transformations and experiencing the fear, joy, and ecstasy that accompany them. Sudden physical illness can give us an awareness of—and an appreciation for—the normal health that we usually take for granted. It can also make us recognize how little is directly under our control. We do not, for example, consciously direct the blood in our arteries to flow at a certain rate or in a certain direction. Indeed, most of us cannot even describe our arteries. We become aware that what we most depend on is outside our control. This awareness, brought about by some change in our normal functioning, can be at once terrifying and liberating—and it can give rise to serious reflection on who we are and how we stand in relation to the rest of being.

We began by reflecting on our relatively simple relationship to our health, but other occasions for insight occur constantly, and we might begin anywhere. We relate to other beings: the insect with a transparent body, the blurred microorganism viewed in a laboratory, the fish leaping unexpectedly out of the water, or the bird whose presence is made known by its haunting song. And we begin to form more complex relationships: not just to the flower we see, but to the flower we care for; not just to the graceful running dog, but to the long-loved, aging pet.

Our relationship to other people is perhaps the most complex. People can mirror us, complete us, challenge us, and free us. Through our relationship to people we can find the most ready access to a spiritual life. Alfred Adler identifies the major problems of life as communal life, work, and love.[1] Each of these challenges provides a context for spiritual insight and spirituality.

LOVE, WORK, AND COMMUNAL LIFE

Love

Love can be observed in many contexts, but we first experience it within the child-mother relationship. The love that a child gets from its mother cannot be reduced to sentimentality or to emotion. First, love means physical caring. But because of the way humans develop, physical caring includes spiritual and psychological components as well. Love, then, is not a feeling or a collection of feelings (we can love while suffering the effects of stomach flu), but a way of living.

What we see in the love of a mother for her child holds for the love between lovers, siblings, friends, colleagues and, perhaps, for the love for all being (what Albert Schweitzer calls "reverence for life"). Any thoughtful exploration of love, whether toward a human, an animal, or a plant, can reveal much about the nature of reality and how we may come into relationship with it. Even love of inanimate objects can provide a way of touching reality: a love for our tools, for instance, or our musical instruments, or the materials through which we express our creativity.

The love that can lead to spirituality is nonpossessive and nonmanipulative, and it transforms the lover and the beloved. It belongs to the domain of freedom, and it makes freedom possible. We can be free because we have been loved, and we freely pass on the gift.

Work

Work is what we do and how we act—the context within which we make our contribution. If we begin with love, we come to recognize that our being and well-being are the result of an enormous gift—our mother's love. Work provides the setting in which we can pass on the gift, making reparation for all we have received. In an ideal world, our work would be what we most need—a way to give. But this is not an ideal world, and so we discover that work can be alienating if we find it dehumanizing or degrading and do not believe in the value of what we do. The meaning of the work is not inherent in the work— it lies in the relationship of the worker to the work. For some people, medicine is an ideal way to pass on the gift. For the less noble, it is a way of extracting further gifts—a means to a material end, rather than an intrinsically valuable practice. Medicine can be life-giving and life-restoring or it can be a means for acquiring status and possessions. Work that is viewed as degrading by some can be experienced as rewarding by those who so relate to it, so it should not be surprising that people who clean cesspools can report that they love their work because it allows them to work outside in nature (which they enjoy) and to help keep this natural world clean.

Another way of exploring the spiritual value in work is in terms of the self-discipline involved. The disciplined training in dance or athletics is similar to that required in many ascetic practices: restrictive diet, "mortification of the flesh," subordination of the body to a higher purpose (ignoring pain for the sake of speed on a track or grace in dance), total concentration, for example. The dedication to work can be harnessed for spiritual development.

Communal Life

Our first experience of community is in the child-mother relationship. In earliest infancy we are unaware of the relationship because we have not yet learned to distinguish the self from the mother who cares for it. Our awareness of the relationship comes about, in part, from the mother's failure to meet some immediate desire of ours. Her failure to respond shows that she is not just an extension of our self but a separate entity. The realization of her separateness grows out of our frustration. Her independence is frightening, but it also makes possible our first love. By her action, which is not merely the anticipation of our own desires, she shows us that she is alive and real.

Some of the ambivalence experienced in this first awareness of community stays with us in all our later communal encounters. We long for the pre-differentiated state of the child-mother relationship, and we long to be submerged in some group where we can substitute "we" for "I." We find that other people are not totally predictable—

that they surprise us. When they do not anticipate our desires, we are frustrated, but we are convinced of their aliveness and reality. If people did only what we wished they would do, if they were merely extensions of our self, we would soon grow uninterested in them. We need them to be alive and real, however scary that might be. There is a sense of community that is not just a harking back to undifferentiated unity but is the fulfillment of all our prior imperfect visions of union. In this sense, community can be our recognition of shared value; it can be our caring for being (reverence for life); it can be our expansion of concern to include larger and larger aspects of reality. In this way communal life can be a context for spirituality.

DE-CENTERING THE SELF

One of the major functions of spirituality is the de-centering of the self. This de-centering can be described in several ways, but the experience in each case is the same. In some traditional writings, the de-centering is called "killing the self." In more modern psychoanalytic terminology, it is called "expansion of the ego boundaries." In the simpler terminology of scripture, it is called "compassion."

When we achieve an integrated self, in the early years of childhood, this fragile self is both an accomplishment and an obstacle. Everything gets referred to the self—all that exists and has meaning or value does so only as it affects the self. As we come to care for people, we care for them only insofar as our self needs them. This perspective creates an enormous obstacle to our perception of people, beings, and ideas. We see only what affects us and perceive things only in terms of their effect on us. But while this shortsightedness is an obstacle and the cause of pain, of acute loneliness, and of repeated disappointments, we feel the pain, loneliness, and disappointment, unaware that it is our concept of self that occasions them. An example, although trivial, may clarify this idea: when we enter a crowded room full of strangers, we might suddenly feel "self-conscious." The self looms so large that it obstructs easy conversation or an everyday task, such as pouring a drink. If we can finally get caught up in someone's story and forget our self, we are freed from self-consciousness and act naturally and with ease. When the self no longer obstructs us, we can enter into other people's concerns with genuine interest. The feeling is expansive—gone is the self's constricting frame of reference. But this ease need not be limited to particular social settings; it can become our fundamental way of being in the world.

Much of the discipline described in traditional spiritual handbooks is structured to foster the de-centering of the self. One method involves overcoming a feeling of repugnance toward something. In other words, if the self has definite preferences, those preferences and aversions must be challenged. In a world view that conceives of the spiritual life as extraordinary, the method of achieving this de-centering is likely to be extraordinary, too. An example can be found in the lives of two saints, Francis of Assisi and Catherine of Siena. Both had very developed aesthetic sensitivities that they sought to mortify by seeking out lepers and embracing them.

It is not clear that the embraces helped the lepers, and herein lies a serious problem. It is surely good to be open to more and more of reality, to overcome narrowness and fear, and to find ever larger areas of sympathy. But when these are achieved by means of an artificial discipline, such as asceticism, there is something unnatural about it. "Bodily asceticism has only a limited use, but true devotion is useful in all things."[2] The de-centering of self achieved through asceticism can be accomplished as well by true devotion, which is first and foremost physical caring. In caring for their infants, mothers don't seek to mortify their sensitivities—they simply know that babies must be diapered and that infants who spit up must be cleaned. They count their action as no great spiritual accomplishment. By merely doing what must be done, their spiritual development proceeds without pride and without strain—it unfolds gracefully.

TRADITIONAL VIEW OF SPIRITUALITY

A quick review of traditional characteristics of spirituality shows that they result from the contexts within which they were formulated. In contrast to Meister Eckhart's admonition to "take your own good way as it comes from God and [believe] that it can include all good ways,"[3] the way that becomes paradigmatic for spirituality is the celibate life within a religious community. The characterizations that result tend to focus on temptations of the flesh and one's response to them (mortification, purgation, fasting, and vigil) and on temptations of the world (that is, of the three domains of human life—love, work, and communal life, as they occur *outside* the religious community). Love is regarded as a recognized context for spirituality, *but* that love is restricted to love of God or love of one's brother. It must be noted, however, that "brother" can refer both to fellow members of the religious community and to humanity in the abstract, but even this "humanity" excludes most members of the opposite sex—that is, women—because of the dangers of "temptation." (In traditional spiritual writings, women represent not fellow human beings but temptation.) Love of parents, of siblings, and of others related by accident of birth is not recognized as a domain for achieving spirituality.

Work is recognized as a context for spirituality, and most ascetics do some manual labor such as planting, baking, or basket weaving. Not recognized, however, is work as it is experienced by those outside a religious community.

Members of religious communities recognize that community plays a major role in spirituality. The importance of the novice's relationship to his spiritual elder is stressed in the writings of the Desert Fathers. There is a significant difference between the spiritual elder and the natural parent and between the religious community and the community in which one happens to live. One chooses one's spiritual elder and religious community because they reinforce and strengthen one's values and commitments. Our natural parents, siblings, and community are given to us and provide a difficult and ongoing experience of learning to deal with "otherness." In both communities, we may transform those around us—and we may be changed. Above all, we must learn to love (be physically and spiritually devoted to) those with whom we are not necessarily in agreement.

By refusing to deny the flesh and instead using it in the service of our devotion to others, we create a different context for examining spirituality—one that yields a healthy corrective to traditional spiritual notions. By refusing to deny the world outside of religious community (the so-called secular world), we allow the bulk of humanity to reclaim the value of the lives they lead with commitment and authenticity. By refusing to pick and choose our community, we arrive at a deeper understanding of the scriptural injunction to love one's enemy.

THEOLOGY OF WESTERN RELIGIOUS SYSTEMS

If we look at prevalent Western religious systems, we see clearly that they result from "insight into the common experiences of *man*kind." God is viewed as male, a perspective that is far-reaching in its implications. The male God is a spiritual (not physical) progenitor and an external judge of creation. Although the term "father" is used, the physicality we associate with fathers is absent from the Western notion of God. The God of Western theology is closer to our notion of artist than of parent. He has "in mind" an ideal form and can judge this world to be in agreement with it or to be flawed. The prevalent notion of God as judgmental is based on the drawing out of the maleness of God. God's own nonphysicality makes the physical suspect, if not absolutely evil. If God, the perfect Creator, creates in a nonphysical way (by word alone), then our nonphysical creations are more divine than our physical creations, theory is held in higher esteem than practice, pure science is nobler than applied science, and procreation is certainly not viewed as a central spiritual experience. The world itself, so material, so physical, and so sexual, is viewed as unreal and as a potential trap for the would-be seeker of God. To achieve enlightenment in traditional Western religious systems, one must be otherworldly.

Once we adopt an otherworldly view, life ceases to be intrinsically valuable—it no longer exists in order to be lived and enjoyed. It becomes instead a means to a goal beyond itself: the achievement of salvation. Life becomes a journey filled with obstacles and traps over which we scramble and struggle in an effort to reach the release from our tainted fleshly existence. Death becomes the entry into a life that is more real.[4]

The essentially judgmental model that denigrates physical being (which is usually female-assigned) has frightening implications for our world. If we are wedded to an ideal form in the mind of God, we can overlook our essential kinship and connectedness with other beings. With grim determination, we subdue our flesh and get on with our solitary struggle for salvation. God's male attributes far overshadow any role of his as father, which would necessitate a prominent role for a mother with whom he has a physical and loving relationship. So we root out of our being any attributes not worthy of our male model.

We do not want to repeat the mistake of traditional writers by insisting that there is but one way to spirituality. Also, any account of reality must at least hold true of our own experience. René Descartes begins with "I think therefore I am" and proceeds to question the nature of this "I" that he is. We, like Descartes, are human, and we can repeat his thought experiment. If the definition of what it is to be human is not true of our experience, then the definition must be false. Our own definition may not be universalizable—we stand in need of other perspectives to arrive at a richer sense of what humanity may be. But even if we cannot generate a final definition, we can at least correct or complement the definitions that currently exist. Similarly, we needn't deny that traditional spirituality can transform selves to bring them into closer relationship with reality. Rather, we can add several contexts, most notably our faithfulness in relationship (to be discussed in chapter 10).

We are trying to relate to reality, but where we locate reality and what we name "real" are major questions of value. To many of the traditional mystics, what is real stands in contrast with—and opposition to—what is apparent in this world. For them spirituality entails the seeker's denial of this world in order to find reality. This world is regarded as a trap that distracts the soul from its genuine objective, the otherworldly reality. One may be worldly or one may be spiritual, but a conjunction of worldliness and spirituality is deemed as contradictory as the notion of a square circle.

Some spiritual writers glory in the beauty of this world and find divinity in and through natural phenomena. They usually are dismissed as "nature mystics" who have achieved their ecstasies in too mundane a fashion (the other world being "on high") and have short-circuited the journey of the soul.

The term "reality" has, in the history of philosophy and theology, been identified with both perfection and being. What this means, simply, is that what is *real* is important—we must take it seriously and pay attention to it. When a child cries out in terror of ghosts or dragons, we reassure the child by saying "ghosts aren't real"—in other words, ghosts have no power, they need not be taken into account, they do not exist. When mystics write "this world is not real," they may be reassuring themselves that there is no significance to what they are experiencing here. They are certainly affirming that their own attention and concern are directed elsewhere. Refusing to bestow the judgment "real" on our world is to trivialize what we do, experience, and suffer in our daily lives. We may endure suffering, but the endurance of suffering is not nothing—it is a triumph that is positively real.

Traditional spirituality has also been characterized as a solitary journey to achieve salvation. The solitary aspect is treated in writings of hermits, anchorites, the Desert Fathers, and the contemporary mystic Thomas Merton, among others. Whether solitude is a good way to achieve salvation is a later question. A prior one is whether there can even be such a thing as solitude. The capacity to be alone is achieved only after one has received the right kind of nurturance. Being alone is not the same as not being in the presence of others; in fact, our first experience of it is in the presence of a loving other.[5] Being alone is, rather, the ability to live out of one's inner life—indeed, to have an inner life. But the inner life that nourishes and sustains the hermits and anchorites was created in relationship to another. We are "alone," but we have with us the language, symbol system, and conceptual tools given to us by society. We fail to recognize that the idea of God that we have formed and the practices that we observe also indicate that we are not—nor have we ever been—alone. Nevertheless, the solitary model persists, together with the equally fallacious notion of the "self-made man" and the myth of self-sufficiency.

Attached to this notion of solitude is the metaphor of a journey to salvation. The idea of a spiritual journey is endemic to spiritual writing. The image of the journey permeates the classics of Western spirituality.[6] The notion of a journey with a well-marked itinerary permeates psychology as well: Daniel Levinson's *Seasons of a Man's Life* and Lawrence Kohlberg's stages of moral development, for example, both presuppose a linear progression with later stages that are valued more highly than earlier ones. The number of stages in Western spirituality varies from text to text. Evelyn Underhill suggests that all the variant maps can be understood in terms of five stages: awakening, purgation, illumination, dark night of the soul, and unitive life.[7] The adoption of the journey model carries with it the view that part of our life has meaning and value only insofar as it contributes to the goal of the journey. Living in itself is not considered intrinsically valuable—the only value is in the goal we supposedly long to achieve. The journey model is not even an accurate description of our experiences—we don't experience our lives in a linear, developmental manner. (This issue will be discussed further in chapter 9.)

Finally, the goal of traditional spirituality is individual salvation, which is understood as union or communion with God. What this means depends in part on where we locate God. If God is outside or above this world, then the salvation must be *from* this world. If we locate God wherever "two or three are gathered in [God's] name,"[8] then salvation keeps us healed and joyous in this world. Nothing indicates that we are here on earth for some goal we may reach— that is, salvation or union with God. We know only that while we are here, there are things we may do that contribute to this world. I believe that we are here to act and to interact with others—to perform, not to escape.

WOMEN AND OTHER "INVISIBLES"

Earlier we considered how insight into the common experiences of mankind constitutes religion. We then saw how religion gives us the jumping-off point for spirituality (coming into relationship with reality). In looking briefly at traditional spirituality and at the mortifica-

tion practiced by Saint Francis and Saint Catherine, we sense that
something unexpected has crept in. We began by stressing the naturalness of the spiritual life and wind up viewing something unnatural,
or at least unusual. How did this come about?

Defining religion as "insight into the common experiences of humankind" doesn't cause this distortion, but its misinterpretation can.
Suppose "humankind" is understood in the narrow sense of "adult
males." Suddenly many people are considered "invisible," and their
experiences are discarded. The experiences of women, children, the
old, or the dying have indeed *not* been incorporated into traditional
Western thinking. A religious system that discounts the experiences of
"invisible people" will be detrimental to the spiritual life of all people. If what some of us experience is not taken seriously, is misnamed
or remains unnamed, and is not given a place in a vision of reality,
three things can happen: (a) we stop having that experience and thereby
lose some of life; (b) we become estranged from our own experience
and live inauthentically; and (c) we contort ourselves in an effort to
make our experience conform to what counts as a "real experience"
in the prevailing system.

In the next chapter we will explore some of women's spiritual experiences, but these are not the only experiences that have been denied. "Unless you turn and become like children, you will never enter
the Kingdom of Heaven."[9] We pay lip service to the significance of
the experience of little children, but in fact their perceptions, their
dependencies, and their prelinguistic beings are rarely explored in
theological systems. When theologians do write of the experiences of
little children, it is not out of the memory of their own childhood or
the research of developmental psychologists, but out of a sentimental-
ized image that belies the intensity of infant feelings. Another example: in some religious systems, followers are exhorted to hold the
image of their death before their eyes. But actual sensitive exploration of the denial, fears, anger, and acceptance of the dying has been
slow to enter the theology. An "image of death" is focused on, rather
than the experience of a relationship with an actual living, terminally
ill person.

If religion is to do justice to our experiences and to foster a relationship to our experience, no experiences can be denied. If religion
is insight into experience but is formulated on the basis of partial
experience only, the insight cannot be whole. Trying to use such a
religion as the basis for coming into relationship with reality leads to
a contorted or distorted life. No one person can have a complete set
of experiences. But a religious system, to be whole, must come out

of such a complete set. It must take into account that we were children—that part of what it is to be human is to have gone through infancy. It must also take into account that part of what it is to be human is to age, to die, to be female, to be rich, to be subjugated, and so on through the endless range of human experience. Only when a religious system provides a larger picture of what it is to be human can we extract sufficient insights to begin to shape our experiences.

Chapter 3

Women and Spirituality

A woman can bring a distinctive perspective to spiritual questions based on experiences that are unique to her. What she requires is a consciousness that will reflect on an experience and not let go until she has understood its value. Many experiences that only women undergo can be quite ordinary, recurring events that reveal nonetheless the nature of reality and shed light on questions of meaning and value. Although women could discount those experiences and still achieve spirituality in more traditional ways, it would be a spirituality lacking an understanding and exploration of their femaleness. Since spirituality, perhaps more than any other area of human endeavor, is the domain of freedom, creativity, and wholeness, it is where we should bring together our most basic commitments. It is also where we suffer the greatest loss if we ignore or deny important parts of ourselves.

Women in most societies have long been relegated to conditions of powerlessness, servitude, and even suffering. To insist that women must derive meaning from their experiences as women in no way justifies or condones these conditions. But people are always more than the sum of what others have done to them. By exercising their freedom and creativity, women can learn even in and from positions of alienation, servitude, and degradation without in any way accepting them or excusing those who brought them about. Women today can compare their perspective to that offered to the Children of Israel in Exodus: "You shall not oppress a stranger, for you know the feelings of the stranger, having yourselves been strangers in the land of Egypt."[1] The Children of Israel are instructed to turn their suffering not into bitterness but into compassion. Women similarly have been strangers and know the heart of a stranger; they too can turn their suffering into compassion and offer unique insights and contributions toward spirituality.

MOTHERING AS A CONTEXT FOR SPIRITUALITY

Women can also contribute to spirituality the insights they derive from their capacity to bear and nurture children. This capacity affords occasions for insight not only into what they can give but into what they must have received. In mothering we recover an awareness that we were mothered, an awareness that many people choose to repress.

What is it to recover an awareness that we were mothered? It is to recognize, acknowledge, and accept that we were once helpless; that the life that flows through us now is a gift; that we were not born strong and masterful, but were dependent creatures who were nurtured by caring parents—obvious points, perhaps, and yet only saints keep that awareness daily before them. Most people want to forget their dependency so they can consider themselves "self-made." To come to terms with one's mother is to struggle to remember something prior to language—to awaken memories that stir in muscles and in nostrils but that cannot be put into words. It is to live a unity that can forever shine through and illuminate all diversity.

> Once again let me emphasize, the result of such recognition of [our mother's] maternal role when it comes will not be gratitude or even praise. The result will be a lessening in ourselves of a fear. If our society delays making full acknowledgment of this dependence which is a historical fact in the initial stage of development of every individual, there must remain a block to ease and complete health, a block that comes from a fear. If there is no true recognition of the mother's part, then there must remain a vague fear of dependence.[2]

We noted earlier that the mother easily accepts the tasks of caring for her infant. This acceptance suggests that mothering—with its complex relationship to another person, its ever-changing roles, and its deep concern, all coupled with vast areas beyond control—may be an ideal context within which to explore spirituality. To do this, however, we must first strike down the prototypical characterization of motherhood in the New Testament, in which Mary's "mothering" consists entirely of serving as a passive receptacle for bearing Jesus. As any mother can attest, this characterization is both inadequate and very inaccurate. Mothering does not end at childbirth, it begins there. Mothering, even in its earliest stages, is not passive. An infant is utterly dependent on its mother—its being and well-being depend on her devotion (physical caring and spiritual involvement). It may be hard for the "self-made man" to accept that he was not self-made, but was nourished, nurtured, cleaned, and burped. It is even harder to picture that the "Son of God" or "Savior" himself needed his diapers changed, his crying comforted, his hunger eased. But spiritual maturity requires that we fully acknowledge our dependence. Long before we were integrated, whole selves, we were enfolded and covered by the integrating force of our mother's love. A passive vessel could not bring forth a living human being, only a living potential human being. If the being is to arrive at humanity, it requires nurturance and care.

To mother is to love, and this is a profound and complex notion in our system. Loving a child does not mean sentimentally gushing over it, it means, first and foremost, physically caring for it. Loving a child also means loving it for itself and not for what it can give to our own self. Mothering entails a species of empathetic, prelinguistic knowledge: to understand an infant is to understand without verbal cues. It is a species of knowledge we would do well to recover. Mothering means learning to let go: the total involvement that is so essential for an infant would be intrusive for a toddler. In short, mothering means de-centering the ego—for a while, the child must come first. Before we can fully appreciate how mothering occasions spiritual insight, we must be clearer about just what mothering is.

The complex enterprise of mothering can be described in its two primary motions: holding and letting go. While holding includes the literal, physical embracing of the child, it is really a shorthand way of referring to much more:

1. Protection from physical harm. This includes the countless daily adjustments to and anticipations of danger: testing the bath water, making sure the infant doesn't fall off the diaper table, etc.[3]

2. Awareness of and adjustment to the infant's sensitivities: the sensitivity of its skin to touch and temperature; its auditory sensitivity to loud noises; its visual sensitivity to bright lights; its sensitivity to gravity (fear of falling).

3. Awareness of and sensitivity to the infant's lack of knowledge that anything exists other than the self. The mother will mediate the world for the infant. Our basic attitude toward the world is fashioned early in the way our mother holds us.

4. Participation in a unique daily routine. It is unique to each mother and her particular child because it is part of the infant, and no two infants are the same. From a spiritual perspective, this is one of the most significant aspects of mothering. The infant is

not yet an integrated individual and is not yet clearly separate from its environment. Part of what it is to be *this* infant is to be in relationship with this mother and this routine of caring. In other words, holding includes integrating for the infant its many confusing experiences by means of the mother's caring concern. Such integration requires the mother's deep knowledge of the infant's experiences. As the infant grows, it claims the experiences and uses them to become a self.

Letting go occurs within the context of the minute, day-to-day changes that mark the infant's physical and psychological growth and development. During the first year of life, the infant moves from absolute to relative dependence. Absolute dependence requires that the mother totally devote herself to the infant *for a limited time.* Any failure of adaptation by the mother can result in serious harm to the infant. The self is being formed during these crucial first months, and the child's capacity to become an integrated unit with a past, present, and future is dependent on this early mothering.[4] But just as total devotion is essential for a short time, it becomes damaging if it persists too long. Minor "failures of adaptation" are needed to allow the infant to see the mother as separate, to learn to signal its needs, to learn to remember the mother when she is not present, and to learn to handle frustration. In other words, the mother must loosen her hold; she must let go of the original closeness and allow the infant to grow. Holding is essential for the infant's being and well-being; letting go is just as essential for the infant's growth.

According to the Midrash (a collection of stories that arose in the Jewish tradition elaborating on the biblical tales and adding others), the sun and the moon were once of equal power and size. Then the moon, saying that a kingdom cannot have two sovereigns, diminished itself so that the heavens would be properly ruled. In reward for her gift of self-limitation and diminishment, she is now accompanied by a multitude of stars, and in herself can take a variety of forms: new, crescent, waxing, full, and waning.

How do we translate this story into our own experience? In the realm of motherhood, we begin as the sun in the world of our offspring. But raising free human beings requires that we voluntarily diminish ourselves and our importance so that our children can eventually rule their own lives. And we, too, will find ourselves accompanied by stars—a multitude of grandchildren and further descendants—and find wholeness in accepting several forms. This voluntary diminishing—an aspect of letting go—complements the motion of holding.

We have all been mothered—and the best evidence for that is our present being and consciousness—but much of the mothering we received was given to us before we had the linguistic or conceptual tools to understand it. When we, in turn, become mothers, we have the possibility, through seeing what we ourselves give, of recovering and finally appreciating what we must have been given.

Traditional writers try to teach us that there is but one way to spirituality: the ascetic life within a religious community. Tradition also applies the term "saint" to those who wear hair shirts, embrace lepers, or fast in the name of achieving spirituality. At the same time, it ignores those whose relation to reality is transformed in the natural course of living out the implications of their devotion. If we trust our experiences while recalling Meister Eckhart's advice to "take your own good way as it comes from God and believe that it can include all good ways," we realize that there are other paths to spirituality. In focusing on mothering as a context for spirituality, we do so not because it is the only way, or even the best way, but because (a) we have all been mothered, so we have had some contact with this way; (b) it is a spiritual context about which traditional writings on spirituality are silent; and (c) by explicitly drawing out the spiritual significance of mothering, we find validity in—and give legitimacy to—what generations of mothers have done, have been, and have experienced.

Mothering teaches us about love: its physical-caring aspects, its knowing aspects, and its capacity to let go. It teaches us how to relate to our mistakes and to the mistakes of those to whom we are connected: "and you will find peace, wisely attaining victory through downfalls."[5] When one helps a child learn to walk, the important thing is the child's learning to walk. The child cannot learn without falling, but to focus only on the falls would paralyze the child and make it incapable of taking risks. So instead, we give support and encouragement for the steps achieved. In seeking spirituality, we reach out to others, and in so doing we also "fall": we make mistakes and inadvertently cause harm. If we focus on our falls, we become frozen in inaction. If we can recognize our fallibility, then with some courage and encouragement, we can once again take risks, go beyond our early mistakes, and "attain victory through downfalls."

The insights that occur naturally in the course of mothering—the need to give oneself over completely, for a time, to the physical and spiritual care of the infant; the need to know by empathetic understanding; the need to endure some limitations (such as sleepless nights occasioned not because of the ritual observance of a vigil, but because a child is ill); the easy acceptance of the natural development through error to correctness; the necessity of loving the child not as a possession but as an independent being; and, perhaps the most difficult insight of all, the necessity of letting go—complement and correct the insights of traditional spirituality.

Traditional spirituality, with its emphasis on individuation, misses the rich spiritual insights inherent in the mother-child relationship. In recovering our awareness that we were mothered, we recover a sense of a nonthreatening helplessness. We need support and nourishment, and we receive support and sustenance on every hand. Traditional spirituality aims at openness and vulnerability but because of its male-centered perspective, it achieves them only by breaking down defenses through artificial trials. Recovering our personal history can achieve the same end more naturally. We cannot come into relationship with reality if we are busy building fortresses.

Looking at our role as mother, we realize that it entails ongoing concern and care. We come into relationship with our child as a result of our daily routines of caring. The spiritual insight that emerges from reflection on this process is that the only reality we can come into a relationship with is one that we are engaged with, that we care about and for. The other process inherent in good mothering, that of letting go, leads us to reflect on a way of relating to our world in a nonpossessive, noncontrolling way.

The concepts of holding and letting go are, in fact, more complex than they appear because our relationships to others change over time. We foster nonthreatening dependency when we recall that we ourselves were once nurtured. Suddenly, the one who cared for us may age and come to need the "holding" that sustained us in our infancy. Our care for the older generation carries with it many of the spiritual challenges we found in caring for the younger generation. But now there is a more radical letting go—giving up our dream of their wholeness and maturation. Although it may be a second occasion for dependency, old age is not a second childhood. We learn to care for and respect another without having any agenda for the one we nurture. And we learn the hardest lesson, which is also the greatest spiritual gift: we learn to see and know with the eyes of love.

Caring is not limited to dependent relationships. In our love for a life partner, we find many of the characteristics evident in parenting and in caring for our elders. Here, too, we must hold, and we must let go. Here, too, we can really know someone only when we are engaged with them and see them with the eyes of love.

All our experiences of caring and of having been cared for, of dependency and trust, and of deep knowing that is nonlinguistic but transformative, find their most essential expression in our relationship to God. Only a growing intimacy with God can allow us to accept dependency with grace and accept the decline of our physical strength with trust. We are capable of loving what death will take away because all our memories and loves are held by God, for, as we read in the Song of Songs, "Love is stronger than death."

So, although parenting may be the most accessible relationship through which many of us can explore our spirituality, any relationship can be lifted up to our covenant with God. (This idea is examined more fully in chapter 10.)

ROLE MODELS

Positive role models can serve to give us a vision of possibilities while negative role models can inhibit and enslave us. For over two thousand years, biblical stories have had a pervasive influence on our culture and on our consciousness. They affect not only our religious thought but our way of viewing art, our social relationships, our responses to nature and, ultimately, our way of understanding our self. Through its depiction of women, the Bible has been used to justify women's subordinate social status and subjugation to men. The few biblical women who have been regarded as heroines either function in traditionally masculine modes, as do Deborah (a judge) and Judith (who decapitates an enemy general), or fulfill a male ideal of femininity, as does Esther (beauty).

The fundamental concepts with which women think about themselves and in terms of which they evaluate their lives have come to them from a one-sided view of experience. It is essential that women understand the role models offered to them so that they may choose in light of their self-awareness rather than in terms of a confused image of who they can become. The role models that men have offered women, even in the case of Esther, conform to a male concept of heroism. Although her mode of success is "feminine" (in the traditional sense of the word) in that she succeeds in terms of beauty, Esther is regarded as heroic because she accomplishes what she sets out to do. Heroism is achieved, traditionally, by accomplishing a goal, by conquering adversity, or by sacrificing oneself for some "noble" cause. But women can choose to redefine heroism in terms that take into account more natural processes. They can opt for a heroism that is achieved by (a) becoming who they are meant to be by being open to those forces that transform them; (b) being able to endure and find nourishment even in the most arid times; or (c) being able to live and to pass on the gifts of life, trust, openness, and the capacity to love. With our new definition of heroism in mind, we can look for biblical countermodels to the Deborahs, Judiths, and Esthers.

It is time to look more closely at biblical women who appear to have failed by men's standards, but who nevertheless are able to remain true to themselves in the face of a harsh, unsupportive environment. Two such women are Hagar and Leah. Hagar, the handmaid of Abraham's wife Sarah, becomes pregnant by Abraham at Sarah's suggestion, is abused by Sarah as a result, bears a son Ishmael, and is finally cast out into the desert and left to die. Leah, grandniece of Abraham, is, through her father's trickery, given in marriage to Jacob, who has just worked for seven years to earn the right to marry her younger sister Rachel, his true love. Leah must endure, one week after her own wedding, the marriage of her husband and her sister. She bears six sons and a daughter, Dinah, who is raped, and serves as stepmother to the two sons of Rachel (who dies giving birth to the younger one). At first glance, Hagar and Leah hardly suggest themselves as role models. Nevertheless, by piecing together their stories from the meager information about them in Genesis, we see that they succeed admirably in transcending such highly unfavorable conditions. Through them we can witness resilience, joy, devotion, and strength.

Hagar

Before we consider Hagar more closely, let us look ahead for a moment at a later story in Genesis.

> Jacob was left alone. And a man wrestled with him until the break of dawn. . . . Then he said, "Let me go, for dawn is breaking." But he answered, "I will not let you go, unless you bless me." Said the other, "What is your name?" He replied, "Jacob." Said he, "Your name shall no longer be Jacob, but Israel, for you have striven with beings divine and human [or God and men], and have prevailed." Jacob asked, "Pray tell me your name." But he said, "You must not ask my name!" And he took leave of him there. So Jacob named the place Peniel ["Face of God"], meaning, "I have seen a divine being face to face, yet my life has been preserved."[6]

This is the formative story from which the Children of Israel derive their name. In the Torah (Five Books of Moses), the only other man to see God and live is Moses, on Mount Sinai.[7]

Now let us look at Hagar's story as related in Genesis. After many years of barrenness, Sarah gives Hagar, her Egyptian maidservant, to Abraham so that "I shall have a son through her." When Hagar conceives, Sarah becomes lowered in her maidservant's esteem, and so Sarah treats her harshly, causing Hagar to run away. An angel of the Lord finds her by a spring of water in the wilderness and tells her to go back to her mistress and submit to her harsh treatment.

> And the angel of the Lord said to her, "I will greatly increase your offspring, and they shall be too many to count. . . . Behold, you are with child, and shall bear a son; you shall call him Ishmael ["God heeds"], for the Lord has paid heed to your suffering. He shall be a wild ass of a man; his hand against everyone, and everyone's hand against him; he shall dwell alongside of all his kinsmen." And she called the Lord who spoke to her, "You are El-roi" ["God of my vision"], by which she meant, "Have I not gone on seeing after He saw me!" [*or* "I have lived after seeing God"].[8]

The parallel with Jacob's story is striking, the more so because the Patriarch's encounter with God is so central to the development of the line of the covenant, and Hagar's is so completely outside it. Both Jacob and Hagar are charged by God with establishing great nations, Jacob through the twelve tribes founded by his sons and grandsons and Hagar through her son, Ishmael. Jacob's story is carried forward in the Torah; Hagar's is abruptly ended.

Hagar's experience of going off into the wilderness is not unique. Many have gone—Jesus, Buddha, the Desert Fathers, Saint Anthony— but they leave behind them a community they can ultimately return to or reject. Some, like the Desert Fathers, even choose to remain in the wilderness. Hagar, on the other hand, flees a community from which she has been entirely excluded. Since she is a woman, the community of ancestry and history is closed to her. Because she is a servant, the community of wives and other women is closed. Abandoned as she is by her "husband," the community of relationships is closed. As the child in her womb faces an uncertain future in view of Sarah's jealousy, the community of legacy and descendants is closed. While others find that the desert experience leads to temptation, Hagar enters the wilderness without any sense of community and—out of this void—sees God.

It is hard at first to reconcile the vision of God, the Great Manifestation, with a return to servitude and ultimate expulsion. Our vision of God has traditionally been associated with the ideas of justice, peace, and paradise. But if instead we associate God with the ongoingness of time—that is, with being itself—then enlightenment is taken out of the realm of the extraordinary. It becomes, rather, an extraordinary perception of the ordinary—of the world we know and inhabit. Such a vision would allow Hagar to return to servitude and submit to Sarah. It does not change the facts of her life, but it profoundly changes her relationship to the facts. Rather than seeing herself as an outsider, as Sarah's slave, she regards herself as a free, enlightened being.

We want the Great Manifestation to be extraordinary, the abolition of all we have ever known. But if this world is the artifact of the Supreme Creator, then it cannot be negated in a vision of God. Human categories that distort creation may be abolished, but the ordinary world is sufficiently extraordinary that to see it really even once is to transform it for all time. When, out of the whirlwind, God shows Job creation, what Job sees is not something novel. He is shown the same creation he knew before (there is only one creation) but from a different perspective. And Job *sees* it, really sees within the world what he had before then failed to see. "I had heard You with my ears, but now I see You with my eyes."[9]

Previously, Hagar had understood her life in terms of the categories that Sarah, Abraham, and the other servants had assigned to it. To see herself suddenly not as their servant but as uniquely herself, one who is precious in God's sight, would allow her to return to her mistress untouched by Sarah's hostility. Hagar finds enlightenment through the very circumstances of slavery and isolation that characterize her existence and that she lacks the power to change. She goes back to the household not to *do* something different but to *be* someone different.

After Hagar returns to servitude, she bears a son, Ishmael. Thirteen years later, God makes a covenant with Abraham, to be carried out through the generations. In return for circumcising every male in his household, Abraham is to become father of a multitude of offspring, who will possess all the land of Canaan. Although God blesses Ishmael and promises to make of him a great nation, the covenant will be kept not with his descendants, but with those of a son to be named Isaac, who will be born to Sarah in her old age.[10]

When Isaac is safely weaned, Abraham holds a great feast to celebrate the occasion. Then Sarah tells Abraham to cast out Hagar and Ishmael, "for the son of that slave shall not share in the inheritance with my son Isaac."[11] Abraham is greatly distressed because Ishmael is, after all, also his son, but God instructs him to do as Sarah says.

Early next morning Abraham took some bread and a skin of water, and gave them to Hagar. He placed them over her shoulder, together with the child, and sent her away. And she wandered about in the wilderness of Beer-sheba. When the water was gone from the skin, she left the child under one of the bushes, and went and sat down at a distance, a bowshot away; for she thought, "Let me not look on as the child dies." And sitting thus afar, she burst into tears.

God heard the cry of the boy, and an angel of God called to Hagar from heaven and said to her, "What troubles you, Hagar? Fear not, for God has heeded the cry of the boy where he is. Come, lift up the boy and hold him by the hand, for I will make a great nation of him." Then God opened her eyes and she saw a well of water. She went and filled the skin with water, and let the boy drink. God was with the boy and he grew up; he dwelt in the wilderness and became a bowman. He lived in the wilderness of Paran; and his mother got a wife for him from the land of Egypt.[12]

Hagar is about to see her young son die, after she had been promised that her offspring would be greatly increased "and they shall be too many to count." Once again it is instructive to look ahead in Genesis to contrast Hagar's story with that of a patriarch, in this case Abraham himself. After Ishmael had been born, God promised Abraham that Sarah would bear a son, Isaac. "I will bless her so that she shall give rise to nations . . . and I will maintain My covenant with him as an everlasting covenant for his offspring to come."[13] But after Ishmael and Hagar had been sent away, Abraham is told by God to sacrifice his son Isaac. Early the next morning, Abraham sets off to do so. Abraham binds Isaac, lays him on the altar, and picks up the knife to slay his son. At the last moment, an angel of the Lord calls to Abraham to stop him.[14]

Both Hagar and Abraham are faced with the imminent death of their sons, after they had been promised that their offspring would be greatly increased. Although the other circumstances in the two stories differ significantly, both sons are saved by God at the eleventh hour. Once again, the patriarch's encounter with God is crucial to the development of the line of the covenant; Hagar, who has a similar encounter, is never mentioned again in the scriptures.

The spiritual insight present in Hagar's story is that of surrender of the self. If we really wish to pass on the gift of life and not view our offspring as mere possessions, we must let go. The desire to hold on even to protect the child becomes an obstacle to the child's independence and its own enlightenment. Letting go in a world that can be harsh and dangerous is extremely painful to a parent, but a gift cannot be held and passed on at the same time. In Hagar's story, the transition has taken place: the angel responds not to the mother's weeping, but to the boy's.

In the desolation of the wilderness, Hagar gains a strength with which to live her life. She also allows the strength to be passed on to an independent offspring. We are unlikely to find ourselves literally abandoned in the desert. The desert, however, is a powerful metaphor for an experience we *are* likely to have. The radical aloneness we face from time to time makes us feel like outsiders to any community. If we follow Hagar as a role model, we use the experience to discover hidden springs of strength.

Certain general categories of experiences may force us suddenly into the desert. As we have just seen, Hagar's social status as woman and slave cuts her off from the community surrounding her. In this she resembles other "invisible" members of societies—the poor, the sick, the young, the aged, the strangers or outsiders—who by virtue of their social status (or rather, lack of status) see the world in ways that others do not.

Other kinds of experiences may project us into the wilderness. For example, our senses may transmit a view of the world that differs from the usual. Such a difference in perception may be due to a physical impairment, such as blindness or loss of hearing. It can also result from a *greater* than usual acuity of sense, where an experience that others find pleasing is perceived as painful.

Another category of experience that can set us apart is that of possessing some basic social anomaly. The late acquisition of speech, for example, lengthens the amount of time during which a person's primary thought processes are nonverbal. Albert Einstein, who did not speak until he was three years old, claims to have understood the special theory of relativity in his muscles two months before he could express it in words and symbols.[15]

Last is the category of experience that challenges our basic thought structures. For example, we may be faced with making a rational choice in a domain where every fiber of our being tells us that the choice has nothing at all to do with reason. In grappling with such a choice, we become aware of the structures that hold rationality together. This awareness forces us beyond rationality into a state of radical aloneness with unshared categories for thinking about reality.

Specific experiences of loss, guilt, conflict, suffering, or pain similarly remove us from the human community. Even experiences of intense joy, love, or ecstasy can set us apart. In our own desert experiences, we can look to the insights of Hagar and derive some help. As long as we retain the vision foisted on us by others, we will remain in the wilderness. The way out of the desert is through creation of a new vision uniquely our own.

Hagar's re-visioning of herself, her identity, indeed her entire reality, sets a pattern that is later followed by patriarchs, prophets, mystics, and would-be mystics down to the present day. In every generation there are those who literally journey into the desert in order to experience for themselves the transformations and insights that the desert occasions. They seek a re-visioning of themselves free of the false self that is fabricated within society. They also seek a vision of reality free of society-bound structures. Superficially, then, Hagar's spirituality resembles traditional spirituality, both in her going off into the wilderness and in her having a vision of God. But Hagar's spirituality differs from that of her male counterparts in four fundamental ways: (a) she begins from a position of weakness rather than of strength; (b) she is thrust into the wilderness rather than choosing it; (c) her focus is always away from the self (onto her child) rather than onto the self; and (d) she learns in the wilderness a way to come *out* of the wilderness and to live in the world community, rather than simply learning a way to live in the wilderness alone or in a carefully selected community of like-minded people.

Leah

Like Hagar, Leah is unloved and is "used" by those around her, even though unlike Hagar, she is very much a member of the family that carries the line of the covenant. Her story as it appears in Genesis is stark, yet each line signifies a drama of intense trial.

The patriarch Jacob, Isaac's son, travels from his father's home to the house of his uncle Laban. He falls in love with Rachel, Laban's daughter and Leah's younger sister, and Laban agrees to give her to Jacob in return for seven years' service. The wedding finally takes place and the marriage is consummated.

> When morning came, there was Leah! So he said to Laban, "What is this you have done to me? I was in your service for Rachel! Why did you deceive me?" Laban said, "It is not the practice in our place to marry off the younger before the older. Wait until the bridal week of this one is over and we will give you that one too, provided you serve me another seven years." Jacob did so . . . indeed, he loved Rachel more than Leah.[16]

In this one paragraph lie the elements of a destructive relationship with Jacob and a lifelong rivalry with her own sister.

Leah awoke on the eighth day after her marriage to Jacob. One week is not very long to win over a husband especially when he has been promised a new bride on the morning after the wedding. Perhaps if she had had a longer time. She looked for a long, thoughtful while at the man lying beside her. He was probably dreaming of Rachel. Love and pain. They had to be compatible. She thought of Rachel, not as she was now, but as she had been so many years earlier—her younger sister, fragile, quick to tears, needing protection. Love and pain. Slowly, quietly, so as not to disturb her sleeping husband, she got up to wash in preparation for her sister's wedding.

What was the night like, the night Leah stood watching her husband of eight days go off with Rachel to his tent? Leah went back alone to her tent. She sent her maid away. Never had she been more alone. She sat in the still darkness a long, long time. Scripture records how Jacob wrestled with an angel. But there is no record of all that Leah confronted that night in the dark silence of her tent.

The Lord saw that Leah was unloved and he opened her womb; but Rachel was barren. Leah conceived and bore a son, and named him Reuben ["See a son"]; for she declared, "It means: 'The Lord has seen my affliction'; it also means: 'Now my husband will love me.' " She conceived again and bore a son, and declared, "This is because the Lord heard [Hebrew *shama*] that I was unloved and has given me this one also"; so she named him Simeon [Hebrew *Shimon*]. Again she conceived and bore a son and declared, "This time my husband will become attached [Hebrew *yillaveh*] to me, for I have borne him three sons." Therefore he was named Levi. She conceived again and bore a son, and declared, "This time I will praise [Hebrew *odeh*] the Lord." Therefore she named him Judah. Then she stopped bearing.[17]

Leah's naming of her sons demonstrates her own desert experience and her slow journey back.

The pain came again. But it was essential to retravel her path through the desert. Reuben. How delighted she should have been with this son. But she never saw him. All she saw was Jacob, his coldness to her. And she thrust aside her first son, naming him to signify "Now my husband will love me." The boy had no way of understanding that he was born to win the affection of a cold husband for his wife. The boy had no way of knowing that his being a first-born would reawaken all his father's guilt about Esau. He had no way of knowing that he was first prize in a contest Leah had with her sister. He cried

lustily. And Leah, lost in the desert, saw only her own distress.
Simeon. Levi. She still cried out to God to resolve her lovelessness.
But after the birth of Levi something was different. Jacob's coldness
didn't change. And slowly she recognized that Jacob would never love
her. When her body rounded for the fourth time she no longer looked
to Jacob for approval. As the tiny son was handed to her she called
him Judah, "this time let me praise God." She had begun the long
journey out of the desert.

It is not Leah, unloved as she is, who becomes jealous of Rachel,
but Rachel who grows to envy Leah.

> When Rachel saw that she had borne Jacob no children, she became
> envious of her sister; and Rachel said to Jacob, "Give me children, or I
> shall die." Jacob was incensed at Rachel, and said, "Can I take the
> place of God, who had denied you fruit of the womb?"[18]

The harshness of Jacob's response to Rachel puzzled Leah. Zilpah
had reported the conversation, and Leah had turned away, unwilling
to face her maid with the pain she felt. It made no sense. Hadn't
Abraham prayed for a son? and Isaac? Why did Jacob not pray on
Rachel's behalf? And the fierceness of his response before the gentle
Rachel: "Am I in the place of God, who has withheld from you the
fruit of the womb?" The barrier between herself and Rachel was gone.
She tried to feel her way through to Rachel's pain. What did she see
when she looked at Jacob through Rachel's eyes? And the tears she
no longer shed for herself she shed for Rachel.

So Rachel suggests he constort with her maid Bilhah, "that she may
bear on my knees and that through her I too may have children."[19]

As relatives of Abraham, both Rachel and Leah might have known
the fate of Sarah and Hagar—that the barren mistress would be de-
spised in her maid's eyes and that the maid's child would not inherit
with the legitimate heirs. Nevertheless, Rachel, in apparent despera-
tion, gives Bilhah to Jacob. She names Bilhah's first son Dan, because "God has vindicated me" (Hebrew *dananni*). She names the
second Naphtali, because "a fateful contest I waged (Hebrew *naphtule*
. . . *niphtalti*) with my sister; yes, and I have prevailed."[20]

At this point there is no apparent reason for Leah to follow suit
and give her maid Zilpah to Jacob, but she does. True, she has stopped
bearing, yet having borne four sons affords her a decided advantage
over her sister's two by proxy, should Leah even consider herself a
party to Rachel's "fateful contest." A possible reason for Leah's action is compassion for Rachel—she knows her sister's pain and chooses

to share in it. There is some evidence for this explanation, as we shall see in a moment.

God heeded Leah, and she conceived and bore Jacob a fifth son, Issachar. And Leah said, "God has given me my reward [Hebrew *sekhari*] for having given my maid to my husband."[21] In Leah's statement we see that she regards her act as a positive one that is worthy of God's reward. We are forced to conclude that she is motivated not by a wish to outdo a rival in a contest, but by a desire to share in the suffering of a sister for whom she feels compassion.

When Leah conceived again and bore Jacob a sixth son, Zebulun, she said, "God has given me a choice gift [Hebrew *zebadani . . . zebed*]; this time my husband will exalt me [Hebrew *yizbeleni*], for I have borne him six sons.[22]

Even after Rachel's maid has borne two sons, Rachel takes the extreme step of turning to Leah, whom she regards as a bitter rival, for help in conceiving:

> Once, at the time of the wheat harvest, Reuben came upon some mandrakes in the field and brought them to his mother Leah. Rachel said to Leah, "Please give me some of your son's mandrakes." But she said to her, "Was it not enough for you to take away my husband, that you would also take my son's mandrakes?" Rachel replied, "I promise, he shall lie with you tonight, in return for your son's mandrakes." . . . And he lay with her that night.[23]

Leah loved Jacob. He did not return her love. They had fine sons, and she loved them. And being bound to her husband through their sons became her first principle. But love knows no first principle. Rachel wanted a son. She wept, she pleaded, and finally asked for Leah's son's mandrakes. Is it possible for us to understand that request—to feel the full force of love that asked the forsaken sister for the very grounding of her first principle? Jacob was her universe. "He loves Rachel, but I have given him sons." And then Rachel, her younger sister, her rival for Jacob, asks for the mandrakes. You marvel that Abraham would sacrifice Isaac to God. Can you marvel any less that Leah would give Rachel the mandrakes?

Rachel finally bears a son, Joseph, then dies giving birth to her second son, Benjamin. She is buried on the road to Ephrath.

Rachel died, and Jacob handed the screaming Benjamin to Leah. And Leah, who had last nursed Dinah, held the infant against her dry breasts. The child sucked and grew quiet. Joseph came over to his aunt. And through the night Leah comforted Joseph and allowed Benjamin to nurse. In the morning Joseph was comforted, and in the morning milk flowed, and Benjamin was nourished. And Jacob built a tower to mark the grave of Rachel. And then he, too, came to Leah to be comforted.

Leah is left to raise the young Joseph and the newborn Benjamin and to comfort her bereaved husband. We hear of her again only to learn that Jacob has buried her in the cave of Machpelah, where the first two patriarchs and their wives—Abraham and Sarah, Isaac and Rebecca—are buried and where Jacob himself asks to be laid to rest.

We find Leah's story compelling because we all feel, at some time or other, that we are not loved enough or that our good deeds do not bring the reward of love. In Leah's situation we might be consumed by jealousy. But Leah not only is not destroyed, she continues to bear children and to impart to them her energy, vitality, and life force. Instead of becoming shriveled up and embittered, she demonstrates true heroism: the ability to endure and find nourishment in a relatively hostile environment and the capacity to be tempered into compassion.

Leah's contribution to a new understanding of spirituality lies in what her life teaches about relationships. Faced with an unloving husband, she does not define herself in opposition to him, but finds a self-understanding that includes him. Faced with a sister who could be viewed as a rival, Leah's response is one of compassion and of identification with Rachel's problems. She defines herself not by separating herself from Jacob, Rachel, or her children, but by understanding her role within this complex structure of relationships. Leah both receives nurturance through her relationships and provides nurturance through them. Through Leah's story we come to understand that a relationship with reality must include all of its aspects.

BEYOND ROLE MODELS

My objective has not been to venerate Hagar and Leah but to use their stories to force us to reflect on female insights into spirituality. One discovery comes from the outsider role that society has thrust on women. While this role is one that women must no longer accept, they can leave it with educated hearts, for now they know the heart of a stranger. We must all struggle to discover who we are, independent of what other people do to us. We must explore our capacity to mother (keeping in mind that this capacity is not limited to women who have borne children, or even to women at all) and recover our awareness that we were mothered. Behind these tasks is our working definition that religion is insight into experience. Our access to this insight must ultimately be through our own experiences and not through those of characters from scriptures. If Hagar and Leah prod us to think about alienation, it is our own alienation, rejection, or estrangement that we are exploring. And if their stories make us aware of the possibility of joy and healing, we must not rest until that experience is our own. In the process of reflecting on our own experiences, we arrive at unique insights that enable us to make a valuable contribution to humanity's spirituality.

Chapter 4

A Spirituality of This World

We have seen how women's experience, especially that of mothering, allows us to have new insights into our relationship with reality. We must now bring this perspective to bear on the concerns that are central to spirituality. Of these concerns the most significant, in its implications for how we live our lives, is how we relate to the world. Traditional spirituality, as exemplified by the lives of well-known mystics, asks us to turn our attention away from this world, this life, and material being, and to focus instead on the "other world." But mothering, whether we are receiving or providing it, makes us intensely aware of this life and of the natural, physical, material world that supports life. The practice of mothering itself affirms this world and militates against otherworldliness—we would not deliberately and joyously mother children if we truly believed the world to be evil or unreal. Yet while we are affirming the value of this world in which we all live, we still hunger after the notion of another world toward which we think we should be directing our attention. This ambivalence in our view can be better understood if we examine otherworldliness more closely.

CONTRADICTORY NATURE OF
MYSTICAL WRITINGS

If we recall the earlier discussion of the theology of Western religious systems, it comes as no surprise to find traditional mystical writings urging denial of this life and withdrawal from this world:

> Seek out places which are secluded and far from the world.[1]

> Do not stay in a town, but persevere in the wilderness. . . . If possible, do not visit a town at all. For you will find there nothing of benefit, nothing useful, nothing profitable for your way of life.[2]

45

As long as the least of creatures absorbs your attention, you will see nothing of God, however little that creature may be.[3]

All the love of this world is based on self-love. If you have given that up, you have given up the whole world.[4]

The Kingdom of God is for none but those who are thoroughly dead [to the world].[5]

But alongside these statements we find others, including some by the same writers, suggesting that the world *is* to be valued. The Anglican mystic George Herbert discovers the sacramental quality of all life and all creation:

> Teach me, my God and King,
> In all things thee to see,
> And what I do in anything,
> To do it as for thee.[6]

Meister Eckhart, who warns us not to allow the least of creatures to absorb our attention, also tells the would-be mystic that "It is not to be learned by world-flight, running away from things, turning solitary and going apart from the world. Rather, one must learn . . . to penetrate things and find God there."[7] He also affirms that "in the work of nature and creation there shines forth the work of re-creation and grace."[8] The contradictory nature of the mystics' writings on how we should relate to this world suggests an attempt on their part to express an authentic experience for which they lack the linguistic tools. In other words, rather than simply contradicting themselves, the mystics are trying to share a positive insight. The following metaphor may help to explain what I mean.

Suppose we lived in a world called Blueland, in which everything is either blue or colorless. Then, one day, we see something red. The concept "red" does not exist in Blueland. We are asked if what we see is blue, and we must answer no. But we also add that what we see is not colorless. What we want to express is something that is both not blue and not colorless.

The mystics' simultaneous claim and denial, affirmation and negation of this world, resembles our attempt to describe a red object in a blue world. Caught up in their world of blue objects, Bluelanders focus primarily on our statement "not blue," just as most people, caught up in this world, find the "not-of-this-world" concept of the mystics startling and memorable. But while "not blue" is true in part, the Bluelanders' assumption of "colorless" misses an important part of our message. Similarly, while mystics *are* in some sense saying no to this world, to assume that another world exists misses an important part of their message. How then can we recover what the mystics really mean in their otherworldly claim?

Since medieval times, nature has been compared to a book that if properly studied would reveal the meaning of life and of our relationship to our source. We are, however, thought to be impeded from "reading" nature in this way by sin. According to Eckhart, "Sinful people . . . are hindered by creature things, enjoying them, each according to his pleasure, instead of God. . . . These people miss their way to God, for even creatures are ways of God."[9] We read in the *Philokalia* that "the primary meaning of the Greek word [*hamartia* ('sin')] is 'failure' or, more specifically, 'failure to hit the mark' and so a 'missing of the mark,' a 'going astray' or, ultimately, 'failure to achieve the purpose for which one is created.' It is closely related, therefore, to illusion."[10] In other words, some illusion or set of misconceptions makes this world—which should provide a way to God—a trap. The otherworldly claim is really a statement not about this world as much as about our way of perceiving or conceiving it.

MEANING OF OTHERWORLDLINESS

Although our context is Western spirituality, Eastern thought can help us understand this otherworldly claim. Buddhism has four "noble truths," the first of which is that life is sorrowful. Yet in all traditional representations of Buddha, Eastern artists show him as either serene, compassionate, teaching, smiling, or laughing—never as sorrowful or weeping. This lack seems to belie Buddha's dictum that life is sorrowful. But Buddha's message is addressed to those who experience life as sorrowful and offers a cure for that sorrow. If life were by its nature sorrowful, the sorrow could not be cured; but if the sorrow resides not in life but in our experience of life, then a transformation of our consciousness could eliminate sorrow. The eightfold path that Buddha offers supports this interpretation. Right view, the first part of the path, is meaningful only if wrong view is the errant path. Right aspiration implies that sorrow can result from not knowing what we may hope for and that if we understood reality better, we would hope only for events that could actually come to pass. Right speech involves carrying our perception to the level of what we communicate. Implicit in these three steps is an ethical dimension: right view—the way we think about the world—is a determining factor in right action. Nevertheless, Buddha adds ethical concerns explicitly: right conduct, right means of livelihood, and right endeavor. Completing the eightfold path, Buddha returns the focus to our consciousness, adding right mindfulness and right contemplation.

Translating this interpretation of Buddhism from East to West, we can regard the claim about the unreality of the world as being addressed to those who experience the world in a particular way. Eckhart gives us a clue to a meaning of otherworldliness. He describes the merchants whom Jesus drove out of the Temple as "good people, working impersonally for God and not for themselves, but they were working under their own limitations of time and number, antecedent and consequence."[11]

CATEGORIES OF THE MIND

Eckhart lays blame not on the world but on a set of categories that mediate between us and the world and color our understanding of it: time, space, number, quantity, antecedent, and consequence. Centuries before Eckhart, the Desert Fathers had already written that we experience not the world but our conceptual image of it. Centuries later, Immanuel Kant caused the "Copernican Revolution" in philosophy by postulating once more that the world itself is never perceived by us and that what we perceive is the appearance of the world filtered through the categories of our understanding. To eighteenth-century minds, that idea was philosophically revolutionary. But the lonely men of the desert, studying the origin of an impulse, inspecting every image and thought, had arrived at the same insight over a thousand years earlier. Saint Maximos the Confessor, one of the Desert Fathers, writes about the natural power of the intellect to form conceptual images. He even contends that evil resides not in things but in the wrong use of our conceptual image of things.[12]

We see now that otherworldliness entails denying not this world but merely one perception of this world. The Desert Fathers' insights grew out of years spent in the desert in careful discipline and reeducation of the self. Living in this world, in families and in intimate relationships, we too can become aware of the categories that interpose themselves between us and reality. Moments—instants free from division and analysis—flash by, but we cannot hold them. There is something truer than our usual understanding of truth, but we cannot find language to express it. The insight slips away, the memory is forgotten or distorted, and our most real moments are dismissed because we have not learned to pay attention.

The categories that obstruct our perception of reality interpose themselves again and again: "As long as one clings to time, space, number, and quantity, he is on the wrong track and God is strange and far away."[13] In forming his epistemology (the study of how we know), Kant rediscovered the concept of categories and concluded that because of them, metaphysics (the study of the nature of reality) was impossible. Reality will always be barred to us, he asserts, because we cannot free ourselves from the categories of the understanding that filter all our perceptions.

Although Kant's insight is the same as that of the Desert Fathers, he arrived at it in a very different context. The Desert Fathers discovered the categories as they tried to analyze the various stages of temptation. In seeking to identify the first seed or germ of sin, they enumerated six stages. The first stage was named "provocation," which Mark the Ascetic defines as "image-free stimulation in the heart." Provocation is a sensation to which we have not as yet applied a meaning. We may have a sensation and then try to determine whether the sensation indicates that we are ill, frightened, or suffering a reaction to too much caffeine. Before we make that determination, we are having a value-free experience: an experience that precedes the categories of our naming and valuing. Our naming or judging the sensation transforms our experience of it. The example of an aroused state, possibly due to illness, anxiety, or caffeine, is analogous to the Desert Fathers' sense of provocation. Because provocation is not yet in the domain of naming or judging, it is value-free, that is, it is not a sin (or a virtue). The experience of something that is prior to naming and judging makes us aware that there is a process or set of categories by which we name and judge. Another stage of temptation is called "coupling," which is entertaining a thought. Should we do it or not? Here, moral responsibility is involved. When the provocation, which was an imageless impulse, becomes a thought, we have allowed the germ to grow and have entered the moral domain, where sin (and virtue) are possible.

The context in which Kant carried out his thinking was significantly different. Kant tried to understand what our minds must be like to be capable of developing Newtonian physics. His categories arose in the context of scientific inquiry and refer to scientific understanding. For Kant, knowledge is exclusively scientific knowledge that allows us to predict, control, or reduce to general categories. When he asserts that we cannot know reality as it is in itself, he is denying this scientific knowledge of reality. But although his context differs greatly from that of the Desert Fathers, his insight accords with theirs.

The Desert Fathers assert that when we are open to whatever impulses occur, we are not in the domain of sin. Only when we take what is prior to images and turn it into thoughts does moral responsibility enter. Kant postulates a reality that is prior to our way of thinking about it. But only when we filter this reality through the categories of the understanding does scientific knowledge enter. Our misconception, our sin, and our scientific consciousness are the subject of otherworldly claims. People who experience the world as an object to manipulate, control, or analyze are the people to whom the "otherworldly" claim is addressed. If that claim is a corrective to a misperception of the world, then scientific consciousness requires an antidote and implies that such knowledge is poisonous. In fact, success in science is as troubling as failure. Kant's great revolution was occasioned not only by the scientific breakthroughs of his day, but by the stark skepticism of his predecessor David Hume. Hume's skepticism was born of triumph, not defeat. Like Kant, Hume was writing at a time of enormous scientific progress. To most of his contemporaries, those advances meant that they had at last come of age—they could understand reality, there was nothing they could not know, and optimism and confidence were the order of the day. A Faustian hunger for mastery is the extreme yet not uncommon response.

But there is another side to the advances: if they were now right, they must have been wrong in the past. Moreover, considering that centuries of great minds grappled mistakenly with the wrong conceptual model, we cannot say that we are right even now—we know only that we were wrong before. From this upheaval all we can salvage is our determination never again to be gullible. If we can comfort ourselves that our mistakes—our unwarranted beliefs—are not after all so awesome, we must admit that our supposed triumphs are not so significant either.

This scenario has been replayed in the twentieth century. While in Hume's and Kant's day a mood of triumph and mastery dominated the age, and the somber countertheme could be discovered only by the perceptive observer, in our age the despair is more apparent. Part of this despair may be due to our failure to know reality, but a larger part comes from our apparent success in knowing reality. A world that we can know (that is, analyze, manipulate, predict, control) is dead. While a living world has the capacity to surprise and delight us, a dead world can offer no comfort, and so we long for another world.

If we are engaged in Newtonian physics, Kant's categories of the understanding are appropriate. In the age of atomic physics, we are forced to concede that the Kantian categories are not immutable. But most of the time, we are not engaged in doing physics at all—we are trying not to analyze reality but to relate to it. It is frightening that the terms in which we describe relationships today all grow out of the Kantian categories (we love in time-bound ways, in quantitative ways, etc.). The spiritual writers' rejection of this world is a positive call for the reversal of these priorities. Rather than understanding love in terms of space, time, quantity, antecedent, and consequence, we are to understand those concepts in terms of love. Rather than accepting the scientific way of perceiving the world as the correct or only way, we can regard it as the way to view the world only when we are engaged in science. When knowledge is restricted to that which enables us to predict, manipulate, or control, the world becomes dead, and we experience life in a mechanistic way. A different sense of knowledge is needed, and this is the crucial insight offered by the otherworldly claim.

KNOWLEDGE IN INFANT CARE

One area in which to seek a different sense of knowledge and a different sense of what is spiritual is in the intimacy of child care. Mothering by its very nature is a denial of otherworldliness. To bring a child into this world is to affirm that this world is a place worth inhabiting. In the first year of mothering we may find a clue to a kind of knowing that is free of the Kantian categories.

The earliest and most striking knowledge that a mother has of her infant is preverbal—infants can offer no verbal cues of their physical or emotional states.

> Actually the word infant implies "not talking" *(infans),* and it is not unuseful to think of infancy as the phase prior to word presentation and the use of word symbols. The corollary is that it refers to a phase in which the infant depends on maternal care that is based on maternal empathy rather than on understanding of what is or could be verbally expressed.[14]

We have all experienced being empathetically understood. It may be that the loneliness—the sense of not being truly known—that some adults experience grows out of a nostalgia for what was once our birthright. As we grow and move into the domains of language and symbols, our mother seems to change the way she knows us. More and

more of our knowledge of one another is transmitted through verbal
cues, until finally our knowledge "literacy" is primarily verbal.

A mother's understanding of her infant affects not only what she
thinks but what she does. Her response is as unscientific as her mode
of knowing.

> The baby does not want to be given the correct feed at the correct time,
> so much as to be fed by someone who loves feeding her own baby.
> . . . The mother's pleasure has to be there or else the whole procedure
> is dead, useless, and mechanical.[15]

In other words, the baby doesn't have simply mechanistic needs
for food, warmth, shelter, and the like. It also has human needs for
relationship—a need that we seem not to outgrow and that may account for our own deadness in relating to a correctly understood but
unliving world.

> The baby appreciates, perhaps from the very beginning, the *aliveness*
> of the mother. The pleasure the mother takes in what she does for the
> infant very quickly lets the infant know that there is a human being
> behind what is done.[16]

The significance of this "aliveness" is not limited to mother-child
relationships. Interaction with other people is fraught with danger. We
wish we knew what they are really thinking and what they plan to
do. We wish they would do what we hope they will do. And yet, should
they become completely predictable and controllable, interest in the
relationship wanes. The relationship becomes simple but dead. A relationship with a human being is dangerous, but it is alive.

FREUD REINTERPRETED

The knowledge required for science can be destructive if transferred
to other areas of our life. To know someone in a mechanistic way is
to threaten the relationship we have with that person. Sigmund Freud
demonstrates in his later writings that he is concerned not with scientific knowledge but with empathetic understanding not unlike a
mother's knowledge of her infant. It is most unfortunate that
Freud's views in this area have been wholly and deliberately misrep-
resented. In a detailed study of the authorized English translations of
Freud, Bruno Bettelheim points out that key terms have been systematically mistranslated in order to emphasize a scientific and mechanistic model that is totally incompatible with Freud's own clear aims.

What was needed was emotional closeness based on an immediate sympathetic comprehension of all aspects of the child's soul—of what afflicted it, and why. What was needed was . . . a spontaneous sympathy of our unconscious with that of others, a feeling response of our soul to theirs.[17]

The mode of knowledge here is love. Previously, knowing had been in terms of the Kantian categories of space, time, quantity, and quality. Now, knowing is meant in terms of the primary category of love. Love, as it is used here, is not a feeling but a category through which we view reality (even as space and time had been categories through which we viewed reality). Feelings are entertained, but we live in our love.[18]

The awareness of a kind of knowing that is not scientific is a crucial insight that came late to Freud. At first, and for a long time throughout his career, Freud maintained that self-knowledge was scientific knowledge, that we could know the rational aspects of our emotions and the repressed causes of our compulsions. Later, through his own openness, he realized that while scientific understanding may be fascinating for the analyst, it may not be genuinely therapeutic for the patient. It was a difficult realization, but he used it to gain a deeper understanding of the self. Freud initially assumed that cures in psychoanalysis were effected by means of rational understanding. If patients were told why they acted in a certain way, then the need to act that way would be dissipated. Consistent with this theoretical model of how psychoanalysts worked, Freud focused on "the facts." He favored hypnotism to bring repressed material to the surface, and the normal course of therapy (in which the therapist did much talking) was a matter of months. But patients frequently rejected the explanation for the illness, or they simply didn't get well. The rational account of the etiology of the illness could be correct, but not therapeutic. Patients did improve, but knowledge of the facts was not the reason. More significant than the facts was the relationship built up in the course of therapy between the patient and the therapist.

THE REPETITION COMPULSION

Freud's conclusion that understanding the reasons for our actions is not sufficient to change them can be explained in terms of his discovery of the repetition compulsion.[19] From the games we play as children to our falling in love again and again with the first object of our love, we have a need to repeat. But therein lies the tension: the repetition compulsion helps us control the world and gives us security, but the price of that security is a kind of death. Recognition that "I've been here before" means "Aha! I can handle it." To the thoughtful person, however, it also means "I didn't handle it completely the first time or I would not be back here again." The optimism, on reflection, gives way to pessimism.

Freud's concept of the repetition compulsion applies on the level of the species as represented in the individual, and on the individual level in terms of one's own life history. Species-wide, we seek to return to an earlier state, the state of inanimate being. This, according to Freud, accounts for the death instinct. Species-wide, then, we fear arousal of tension, stimulation, and novelty. Individually, we deal with novelty and arousal by returning again and again to childhood modes of dealing with threat. By repeatedly acting out our earlier response, we feel that we are enacting the response as opposed to merely suffering it. Our former passion becomes an action, and we have controlled the frightening situation. The repetition compulsion, while apparently natural, can become obsessive. It could not of itself account for the cure in therapy. Merely reliving earlier traumatic situations in the presence of a therapist would not be curative, were there not some additional factor that allowed the reliving to differ decisively from the original experience. This additional factor is the principle within the living being that fights the death instinct. Freud identifies this life instinct as Eros.

Freud's understanding of the repetition compulsion applies not only to us as a species and as individuals, but to Freud's own writings as well. Faced with a demand for freedom but aware that everywhere humans are enslaved by their emotions, compulsions, and obsessions, Freud chooses essentially the same solution as did the stoics and the rationalists before him. He identifies the rational component within emotion, but concludes that this rational analysis does not provide mastery over the emotion. In this regard, his own work rediscovers the insights of his predecessors. The patient's capability for growth and liberation increases with the awareness that what appears to be reality is in fact only a reflection of a forgotten past. Similarly, Freud's awareness allowed for growth in his system and liberation from past theoretical models.

If there were only one principle operating within humans—the conservative instinct that thwarts all change, growth, and tension—we could not account for human life. The second principle, Eros, not only challenges the death instinct, but accounts for the contradictory impulses within people. Freud concedes that many of his readers may find his postulation of Eros "positively mystical." Like the repetition compulsion, Eros functions for the species through individuals and for individuals through their life experiences. It is the latter process that concerns us with regard to psychoanalytic theory. Patients learn to understand their responses not by means of a rational, cognitive process but through a deep emotional commitment to the therapist. This is a direct extension of the Platonic idea that all true learning occurs through love.[20] The cure effected by the psychoanalyst is not based on the analyst's unique characteristics but on the transforming power of love. This growing recognition of the centricity of love is the thread that joins together much of Freud's later writings.[21]

THE INNER OTHER WORLD

The mystics have proclaimed to us another world—not one that can be located in space but one that is known through love. This mode of knowing, central to Buddhism, to the Desert Fathers, to Eckhart, and to Freud, is the ordinary experience of most mothers in the daily care of their infants. Two additional factors must be considered in an examination of otherworldliness: (a) our *experience* of another world and (b) what it is that leads us to value another world above this world. Let us return to infant care to see how external reality is presented to us and how inner reality is nurtured.

> Imagine a baby who has never had a feed. Hunger turns up, and the baby is ready to conceive of something; out of need the baby is ready to create a source of satisfaction, but there is no previous experience to show the baby what there is to expect. If at this moment the mother places her breast where the baby is ready to expect something, and if plenty of time is allowed for the infant to feel round, with mouth and hands, and perhaps with a sense of smell, the baby "creates" just what is there to be found. The baby eventually gets the illusion that this real breast is exactly the thing that was created out of need, greed, and the first impulse of primitive loving. . . . A thousand times the feeling has existed that what was wanted was created, and was found to be there. From this develops a belief that the world can contain what is wanted and needed, with the result that the baby has hope that there is a live relationship between inner reality and external reality, between innate primary creativity and the world at large which is shared by all.[22]

We learn to trust the environment through the adaptation of our mothers to our needs. Minute failures of adaptation, as we get older, help us to distinguish between inner and external reality. Why, then, do we ever turn away from external reality to our inner or "other" world? We do so when external reality becomes too painful, and we wish to flee from it. The temptation to flee is real but strongly argued against in traditional Judaism. The argument takes the form of a commentary on the story of Moses' vision of the Burning Bush. Moses "gazed, and there was a bush all aflame, yet the bush was not consumed. . . . And [God] said, 'Do not come closer. Remove your sandals from your feet, for the place on which you stand is holy ground.'"[23] Why is taking off one's shoes the appropriate response to standing on holy ground? In traditional Judaism, there are three occasions when adherents are prohibited from wearing leather shoes: during the week of mourning for the death of a next-of-kin, during the communal mourning for the destruction of the Temple, and on Yom Kippur, the solemn day of atonement. It is explained that on each of these occasions we are tempted either to flee from our sorrow (during mourning) or to flee from the secular world (on Yom Kippur). For this latter reason Moses is told to remove his shoes. The temptation is to flee, but the commandment is to feel the ground under your feet. Here, where we truly stand, we must bring in the holy—we must not fly to it. Here, where the pain of death makes us want to quit this world, we must feel this world's reality, its physicality, its materiality under our feet. The best response to otherworldliness, then, is to explore those situations that make it difficult to put full commitment in this world.

Chapter 5

Circumstance, Conflict, Suffering, and Guilt

When we examine the appeal that another world holds for us, we discover the fears we have about this world that make flight attractive. Fear is common to all of humanity. Some women, through their experiences, have achieved important insights into fear that allow them to affirm this world by raising children. Others have succumbed to fear and seek to flee this world. Such flight can take the literal form of running away from human contact. More often it takes the form of agoraphobia (fear of open spaces), depression, or addiction to alcohol and other drugs, all of which are conditions suffered primarily or increasingly by women. It is a paradox that some women flee the world by wrapping themselves in it. Instead of experiencing a deep encounter with reality, they distract themselves by interminable busyness. Since it is not experience itself but insight into experience that leads to religion, a life structured so as to leave no time for reflection is a life of flight.

Karl Jaspers contends that the fearful situations that drive people to seek another world define the human condition. "Situations like the following: that I am always in situations; that I cannot live without struggling and suffering; that I cannot avoid guilt; that I must die—these are what I call boundary situations."[1] Dunne refines and restates the notion: "Inside the human circle as it stands there are the tasks of life, love and work and communal life. Outside it there are the boundary situations that define the human condition, circumstance and conflict and guilt and suffering and death."[2]

The fear occasioned by these "boundary situations" lies behind our attraction to another world. The other world of traditional spirituality would allow us to weed out or reinterpret the threatening situations that cause fear. For example, the loss incurred by death is viewed as the joyous entrance to the real life. The boundary situations are no less threatening to women than to men, but in the course of mothering, women's experiences offer alternative responses to these threats. If we are committed to this world, we do not look for a solution in another world. If we are committed to the wholeness of those for whom we care, we cannot weed out or uproot aspects of our being. If we are committed to life, we cannot help but mourn death. What we *can* do is explore ever more deeply, in light of the experiences of mothering, the situations that define the human condition. We will see that the spirituality that emerges from such an examination is life- and world-affirming. It is focused not on fear but on trust.

Our study of the boundary situations begins with explorations of circumstance, conflict, suffering, and guilt. In chapter 6 we will look at the problems presented by death. In each case, we will see that what traditional spirituality puts in a negative light can be interpreted positively when women's experiences are taken into account.

CIRCUMSTANCE

Circumstance encompasses the influences on our life that are beyond our willful control. An awareness of circumstance carries with it the realization that our being and well-being are not guaranteed. We may become conscious of circumstance only when something we never think about goes awry. Let us say that one of the many blood vessels that we take for granted ceases to function. Nonbeing suddenly looms as a real possibility. Long after the blood vessel has been cleared, and the blood again circulates normally through our system, thoughts of nonbeing and meaninglessness reverberate in the mind. Until we conclude that what we cannot control is nonetheless controlled, and until we come to trust this control, our experience of circumstance is one of terror.

Circumstance is experienced as the unpredictable and—more important—the uncontrollable. We cannot control the circulation of our blood, the action of viruses, the events that cannot be explained by a general law. The actions of other people, in their independence and otherness, demonstrate repeatedly how much we cannot control. The awareness that we are unable to understand and explain all reality in terms of our rational categories leads us to fear for our very lives. But in the face of this fear in the context of circumstance, we can discover something of positive value. We realize that although we cannot control our being and well-being, our being is not uncontrolled, and we begin to discover the gifts that nurture and sustain us. This idea lies at the core of a statement by Anthony Bloom: "Poverty is the root of perfect joy because all we have proves love."[3] The term "poverty" immediately brings to mind an economic condition. This association demonstrates how all-pervasive and influential the category of quantity has become. But the poverty that is the root of perfect joy is not economic. There is an awareness open to all, wealthy or destitute, that whatever we possess is never ours—that everything to which we lay claim is a gift. We did not create our own being (the myth of the self-made man notwithstanding), nor did we create that on which our being and well-being depend. Poverty may bring about terror, but it also opens us up to joy. If everything is a gift—a concrete expression of God's continuing, sustaining love—then poverty affirms our ongoing relationship to God in a way that possession never can. Now circumstance provides evidence of love.

Circumstance, for all its fearsomeness, also demonstrates vitality. As noted earlier, a mechanically regulated world estranges us. With each advance in science, from the time of Aristotle to that of nuclear physics, the initial optimism brought about by our increased understanding and control has given way to a feeling of isolation. If the world is seen to be mechanically ordered, it is not alive and cannot respond to us. In an unfeeling world, we feel alone. But coming to understand the world need not lead to estrangement from it. Only when "understanding" is taken to mean relegating the observed phenomena to the various Kantian categories is one left to analyze a dead object. When "understanding" means empathetic identification with the world, it leads inevitably to a relationship with the subject—and to wonder. Einstein the agnostic became Einstein the theist out of wonder at the beauty of the universe. Our way of looking at the world (as object or as subject) determines our relationship to it.

Most philosophers in the Enlightenment were atomists, and believed that all of reality was no more than the conjunction of infinitesimal pieces of matter. These bits of matter, they held, comprise not only our physical world but our intellectual world as well. All our thoughts and imaginings are fashioned out of bits and pieces of what we have experienced in the physical world. The occult entities that had been so necessary before Newton's time to explain "action at a distance" (action without contact between two related events) were no longer needed once the laws of gravitation were formulated and generally accepted. Similarly, the occult entity used to explain combustion was no longer needed once oxidation had been understood. Little by little, the world yields to our probing, the mysterious becomes the manageable, and the concept of an unseen, unknown transcendental disappears. At first such a view of the world appears to be an optimistic one, because if there is no higher reality telling us how to live our lives, then we must be free. But further reflection shows that the view really covers a deeply felt pessimism. While the higher reality might be, let us say, a stern judge, its presence does guarantee the reality of caring concern and a world that is personal. Without the higher reality we are left free, but with a dead, impersonal world.

Along with our awareness of circumstance comes a renewed experience of aliveness. The universe can now be experienced as a party to a living, mutual relationship. We come to know that the world is more than a mechanistic system because we have experienced its aliveness, both in those areas that we cannot control but that are nevertheless controlled and in the areas that surprise and delight us. The uncontrollable world may subject us to experiences of disequilibrium and turmoil, but these are a small price to pay for creativity and growth. Life entails risk—the safe world of the mechanist is safe only because it is dead. Fear of circumstance is not to be fled from but entered into. By fully experiencing and exploring it, we emerge with a deeper trust for reality—not trust only in what we can control but trust in a living relationship.

Motherhood provides women with a special context for experiencing circumstance. Tremendous changes in the body during the months of pregnancy occur with overwhelming rapidity. A pregnant woman's happiness is inextricably connected with the well-being of the life forming within her, yet most of that developmental process is beyond her control. She grows impatient for the birth to verify that the baby is normal, while at the same time she knows that every day of gestation is important for her child's well-being. When the child finally is born, she counts the fingers and toes, almost unable to grasp that she has given birth to someone as wonderful and perfect as this! It is hard to go through pregnancy without being assailed by fears of illness, deformity, or death. Most women, however, go beyond these fears to joy—a joy deeply rooted in trust.

The fear involved in mothering does not end with a normal delivery. On the first day away from the reassuring context of doctors, nurses, and experienced mothers, the new mother is struck by the infinite value of her baby and the fragile grasp it has on life. Will it continue to breathe even though she cannot control it? The wonder that the infant arouses in the mother initially produces fear, but the fear gives way, at last, to joy.[4]

The mother's trust must extend not only to the being and well-being of the life that is developing within her and the being of that life when it is now outside her, but also to the otherness and independence of that life as the child moves from infancy to childhood. Being able to move beyond fear in allowing the child to become independent is to trust fully that one can "take your own good way as it comes from God and believe that it may contain all good ways."

CONFLICT

Conflict occurs first within ourselves. Our reason, emotion, and action do not always agree. Buber suggests that this internal conflict lies at the heart of our other conflicts. In order to solve them, he advises, "Seek peace in your own place."[5] We experience conflict with other people and, finally, we feel in conflict with reality itself. It does not conform to our wishes, nor does it seem to offer a context in which we can realize our dreams. All these conflicts occasion fear, but if we can go beyond fear, we can transcend conflict.

Our internal conflict is produced by the fear that in living our life we must deny a part of our self. For example, our emotions are so strong that we fear they may overwhelm our reason, but to deny our emotions is to lead a heartless life. Also, we face decisions daily that appear to require choosing one action and rejecting many others, which results in a fear that we are missing something.

Were we to enter into the fear rather than trying to escape it, we might find a way to achieve unity, accord, and peace. Behind the notion of "entering into the fear" lies the belief that "fear is a high energy state that, true to this pattern, wants to come to completion. Therefore you don't explain fears away, you experience them, you integrate them, you let them go to their end."[6]

The fear that we may be missing something is based on false assumptions, all of which may be traced to the Kantian categories of the understanding. If we start with a mode of thinking based on time and quantity, we assume that all our time must be directed toward our goal (whatever it is) and that we must not digress from our path to that goal. At the same time, we fear that one road offers a richer life than another and that we have no criterion for choosing one over the other. Eckhart suggests a solution to this conflict: "All people are not called to God by the same road. . . . Whatever possibilities inhere in any pattern of life inhere in all, because God has given it so and denied it to none."[7] He advises explicitly, "Whatever the way that leads you most frequently to awareness of God, follow that way."[8] Eckhart stresses over and over that we each have our *own* way and that our task is not to rule out choices but to find which way most belongs to us. Buber expresses a similar view in writing of "God's all-inclusiveness manifest[ing] itself in the infinite multiplicity of the ways that lead to [God]," each of which is open to us. Buber contends further that the way by which we can reach God is revealed to us only "through the knowledge of [our] own being, the knowledge of [our] essential quality and inclination."[9]

Our fear with respect to reality is that finally it will not support us—that were we to put full weight on this world, it would let us down. William James argues that "faith in a fact can help create the fact."[10] If we accept this idea, then withholding faith and trust estranges us from the world and makes it incapable of meeting our deepest needs.

The conflict we experience within ourselves, in our choice of action and in our relationships to others and to reality, can be overcome by a choice against fear—a coming to trust. As mothers teach their children to let go in the nightly struggle against sleep, they are reminded of their own need to let go. As they try to get the shy toddler to meet the world halfway, they remember their own need to be more open to and welcoming of the world. As we teach our children to deal with conflict, we teach lessons that we ourselves need to relearn. Motherhood affords the opportunity of reliving childhood, of becoming "as little children," and in the process, of acquiring *with consciousness* a way of being that was formerly unconscious.

Sometimes in child care we experience a tremendous simplicity, which is in reality the resolution of conflict. When the conflict has been an internal one, the resolution is felt as wholeness or being at one with every aspect of our self. When the conflict has been with another person or with other people, its resolution brings a feeling of accord. When the conflict has been with reality, its resolution is experienced as peace. Because the resolution of conflict is simple and natural, it may not be properly noted and valued. People may be looking for flaming cherubim when the resolution may be in the simple, natural delight of enjoying other people more or feeling more at peace with others. The experience is unspectacular but not unfamiliar:

> And with the morn those angel faces smile
> Which I have loved long since, and lost awhile.[11]

This peace, this simplicity, is what we long for in the midst of the anguish of division.

SUFFERING

"We suffer in so far as we are a part of Nature, which part cannot be conceived by itself nor without the other parts."[12] We are a *part* of nature, not the whole. Our incompleteness leaves us open to what we cannot control—that which can cause pain and loss. Our awareness that we are a part dependent on the whole comes to us in several ways. One that we have already explored is circumstance. Another way this awareness comes to us is through sex.

If we look for completeness on the level of the material body, we come to the disturbing realization that we are not complete individuals. The sex organs are central precisely because they point so conspicuously to our incomplete nature. The full definition of what it is to be a table may be embodied in any particular table, but there is no person—nor can there be—who embodies what it is to be human. Our incompleteness helps define our animation; in our incompleteness we are alive. Our yearning for wholeness, our reaching out to others, our love—that is the life force.

"I" and "We"

The self as animate, then, is incomplete, reaching out for that which would complete it and make it whole. A self that would be complete might be named "we" rather than "I." But who is this "we," and how do we come to know it and relate to it? Our access to the "we" is immediate both through our own being and through our interaction with the external world. "We" is not only outside and around us, it is at the innermost core of our being. When we try to discover what is most intimate to us, we systematically strip away those things that seem most removed from our essential nature. At the most external level, the self is physical. But while we clearly identify ourselves with the physical self, we think that people who knew us merely as a physical self would know us in no more significant sense than they knew a tree or a table. We *are* physical objects, but we are so much more, though we find "we" reflected in the physical self. Our mannerisms and gestures are nurtured and formed in culture.

More intimate to the self than the body is the intellect. But as we scrutinize the intellect, we discover that its language is the language of community, its values grow out of society, and in fact all its symbols and criteria of validity are composed of shared elements of "we." Closer still than the intellect is the experiencer—the ego. At this most personal level of self we discover, once again, "we"—it is the common conception of reality that goes into the formation of the ego. And if we strip away yet one more level of self, more intimate even than the ego, we discover the most profound sense of "we." Now "we" is not limited to a particular culture or tradition but is being itself, which unites us with all that is. At the core of our being, stripped of all cultural accretions, we are more clearly "we" than even culture itself attests. We are individuals—being is always manifested in particular beings. But the more closely we know the self in its uniqueness and idiosyncratic particularity, the more we know about being in its universality.

One way to deal with suffering is to move from the care for beings to "the care for Being."[13] Our suffering comes from the fact that "we are *a part* of Nature, which part cannot be conceived by itself nor without the other parts." How do we go beyond suffering? Not by fleeing this world but by expanding our concern to include more and more of the world. Expansion of the ego boundaries, which has sometimes been referred to as the killing of the self but in simpler terms is the gaining of true compassion, frees us from "the privateness of private fortune and misfortune."[14] This process can, by itself, overcome suffering.

Mothering gives us a special perspective on incompleteness and on that which we cannot control. The fetus, in utero, is both the self and other. The mother identifies with it and yet is aware that its sleep pattern may not coincide with her own. In fact, often when the mother is still, preparing to sleep, the fetus is most active, forcing on the mother's awareness a realization of its otherness. During all the stages of childhood, there is the curious tension between deep identification with the child and growing awareness of its separateness and otherness. Suffering comes when identification obscures the reality of otherness or when the fact of otherness severs the bond of identification. Mothering teaches us to care for our children not as belonging to us, but as belonging to themselves.

Pain

Pain hurts. Yet we cannot conclude that it is evil or that the world containing it is evil. Rather, we must explore what use we can make of it. One way to do this is to examine what happens to people who are unable to feel pain. There is a physiological condition in which the nerves fail to transmit pain messages. People afflicted with this condition cannot feel when their hands are subjected to extreme pressure, heat, or other damaging forces. The inability to feel pain makes these people highly vulnerable to severe injuries. Pain often serves as a vital signal. It tells us to see a doctor, not to push so hard, or to take a nap. But sometimes it seems to persist beyond the useful level of signalling, as in cases of terminal illness.

Pain consists of two components: a physiological sensation, followed by our interpretation of it. When the dentist puts a mirror instead of a drill into our mouth, we may experience the pain of drilling anyway because we anticipated it. Our pain in that situation is due to our (faulty) expectation. Terminally ill cancer patients in hospitals typically receive pain killers, often in dosages so high that the patients are not fully conscious. Terminally ill patients in hospices, on the other hand, are physiologically just as ill but can rely on drug dosages of a much lower order.[15] Pain is related to our anticipation of it, our interpretation of it, and to the many unanswered questions that the pain itself raises. An enlightened approach to pain management may actually lower the experience of pain if it (a) anticipates and treats the pain before a patient can come to expect it, thereby eliminating the anticipatory aspect of the pain, and (b) answers the patient's questions and fears and gives attention to the patient even when he or she is not in acute distress. So pain in the terminally ill may be a useful signal, alerting the patient and health-care professionals as well as others close to the patient that questions remain. The patient needs to talk, to be visited, to have some sense of giving, and probably needs some help in making sense of her or his life.

When we experience pain, our first instinct is to flee from its source. But pain is real and demands our deepest compassion and understanding. Therefore, we should not respond by immediately fleeing to another world, but by exploring our own world more deeply and discovering what the pain may signal.

The insights we derive from the terminally ill on pain interpretation and management are confirmed by women reporting on childbirth.[16] The Lamaze method of prepared childbirth (also called the psychoprophylactic method) has as its major premise that stimuli can be interpreted according to conditioning. Since most women in Western cultures have learned from the Bible that they must bring forth children in pain and have heard labor contractions referred to as labor "pains," they will probably interpret all sensations relating to labor as pain unless they are reconditioned. People trying to explain the lack of pain in the labors of "reconditioned" women have done so in terms of modification of stimuli, rather than change in interpretation. They claim that the new breathing techniques make the labor more efficient and hence less painful. Yet there is one stage in labor, called "crowning," for which no action on the part of the woman is prescribed in any method of childbirth (therefore breathing techniques could not be a factor). In most books on the physiology of labor, writers warn that "This is the time when you will most want anaesthesia," or, "If it weren't such a short stage, it would probably be unendurable." Some women writing of their experiences seem to verify this, describing it as the most painful experience they have ever suffered. By contrast, women who have prepared for childbirth by the Lamaze method invariably describe this *same* experience as intensely joyful and as the most pleasurable sensation they have ever had. In other words, the same stimulus is subject to interpretation as either pleasure or pain. It is not the particular *feeling* (pleasure or pain) that is being interpreted. If it were, it would be open to misinterpretation, and one could say, "You're mistaken, you are not in pain." Rather, certain cues are subject to interpretation. For the untrained woman, the beginning of a contraction is a cue to experience pain. She tenses her muscles in expectation of pain, and her threshold of pain perception lowers. When the contraction is painful, she is not mistaken in reporting her pain. She was perhaps mistaken in interpreting the onset of the contraction as a cue to expect pain, but once she had a "mental set" to experience pain, her assertion concerning the sensation of pain cannot be questioned.

The significant difference between the woman prepared for natural childbirth and the woman unprepared is one of attitude—the difference between trust and fear. Fear heightens pain perception and leads the expectant mother to fight against the process of labor instead of cooperating with it. Trust leads to a reinterpretation of the stimuli and a letting go of one's own control for the sake of the higher control that is bringing the baby forth from the body.

Loss

"But all good things must come to an end, as the saying is. It is part of the good thing that it ends."[17] We love the infant's total dependence in part because we know it contains within it the seed of independence. The infant that stayed an infant forever would not be a joy but a tragedy. We love the intensity of gazing in our lover's eyes, but in a few minutes the gaze has shifted. If it did not, our world would be severely limited. Inherent in all our deepest joys are natural limits: "A setting sun sets; a vision from a mountain top ceases; lovers do not stay in bed forever; a symphony has an ending. . . . Life itself has its ending and its limits, as do all the joys within life."[18] Once again, Eastern thought provides insights that make this point clearer. Representations of Buddha differ significantly in the position of the hands. One traditional statue shows Buddha seated in the lotus position. His left hand rests on the ground in recognition that he is rooted in the earth, and his right hand is open, slightly cupped, allowing for all that comes to be accepted. Nothing is grasped or held. To recognize our deep connection to the world and to accept what is given to us without clutching at it is to move beyond suffering.

GUILT

When we think about guilt, we think about ideals we have failed to live up to or values we truly hold but cannot consistently maintain. Such guilt appears to be a rather late maturational accomplishment, and the inability to resolve it makes another world, with its implicit notion of a second chance, seem appealing. Yet we have strong evidence that guilt is not foisted on us by society, but develops naturally within the first two years of life, and has a natural solution.

> [Melanie] Klein has developed the idea, however, that the primitive love impulse has an aggressive aim; being ruthless, it carries with it a variable quantity of destructive ideas unaffected by concern. These ideas may be very restricted at the beginning, but the infant we are watching and caring for need not be many months old before we can be fairly certain that we can perceive also the beginnings of concern—concern as to the results of the instinctual moments that belong to the developing love of the mother. If the mother behaves in that highly adaptive way which may come naturally to her, she is able to give plenty of time for the infant to come to terms with the fact that the object of the ruthless attack is the mother, the same person who is responsible for the total infant-care situation.[19]

In other words, when the infant feels the tension of hunger and observes the breast, it attacks the breast in a desire to satisfy its hunger. In its quieter moments, when the hunger has been appeased, it begins to gradually recognize that the breast it had attacked belongs to the mother who gently holds it. The guilt experienced by the infant is resolved in two ways. First, the mother survives; the intensity of its feelings did not destroy her. This allows the infant to accept responsibility for its feelings. Second, the infant needs an opportunity to make reparation. As the mother acknowledges and accepts the restitutive gesture of the infant (be it a smile, a gentle stroking, or a cooing), the infant can work through guilt and move from unconcern to concern. What seems clear from this developmental account of a sense of guilt is that "a child needs to give even more than to receive."[20] The need to give does not end with childhood. When Elisabeth Kübler-Ross asked terminally ill patients to submit to interviews, more than 98 percent agreed. In analyzing why so many of the patients were willing to share their experiences, she writes:

> Many patients feel utterly hopeless, useless, and unable to find any meaning in their existence at this stage. . . . Another aspect which is perhaps more important is the sense that their communications might be important, might be meaningful, at least to others. There is a sense of service at a time when these patients feel that they are of no earthly use to anybody anymore. As more than one patient put it: "I want to be of some use to somebody. Maybe by donating my eyes or my kidneys, but this seems so much better, because I can do it while I am still alive."[21]

We need to give even more than we need to receive. The answer to guilt, then, is not to flee from this world but to turn to it, with loving concern, to discover the contribution we can make to it. We are here "for the sake of the work which [our soul] is destined to perform upon the world."[22]

Original Sin

When the new mother views her infant and counts the little fingers and toes, she knows that what rests in her arms is perfect. If we begin from the position that religion is insight into the common experiences of humankind, we must ask what experience gives rise to the doctrine of original sin. Certainly the mother's experience of her newborn child does not suggest such a doctrine. Mary's prayer of thanksgiving for the coming birth of her child, based on Hannah's prayer in the Hebrew Scriptures, seems a clearer expression of the mother's joy:

> My soul magnifies the Lord,
> And my spirit rejoices in God my Savior.[23]

One insight in the doctrine of original sin is rooted in our experience of mothering. According to tradition, the sin that led to Satan's fall was pride. Kafka writes that the root of all sin is impatience.[24] Al-Hallaj contends that the sin of jealousy caused Satan to fall.[25] Behind each of these concepts—pride, impatience, and jealousy—lies fear. Jealousy is but the fear that there will not be love enough, impatience the fear that there won't be time enough. Pride is but the fear of admitting that we are not self-made—that all we possess is evidence of love. Saint Maximos the Confessor characterizes fear as "an evil which is expected in the future."[26] In discussing the fear of God, Saint Diadochos of Photiki adds: "The soul is gradually cleansed until it is completely purified; its love increases as its fear diminishes, until it attains perfect love, in which there is no fear."[27]

From this statement we deduce that fear is what stands in contrast to love and that fear is the root of sin. A mother can come to these insights by observing her children's development. The doctrine of original sin grows out of the inevitable movement from trust to the breakdown of trust, or fear. In infancy our being is supported by the love of others; we have not even reached a level at which we can formulate the notions of "others" or "separate." We are supported, and we rest in that nurturing environment. With the awareness of otherness, however, comes an awareness and fear that what was given could be withheld. Rather than centering on the "given" aspect, we focus on the fear. We approach our environment warily—we begin to test. But testing reality changes it. When we cease to know with absolute certainty that we are loved, we change our relationship to our self, to our parents, and to reality. When we are no longer sure that nothing will be withheld, we grasp and thereby distort the freely given gift. What makes us demand tokens of status, wealth, or fame is our lack of trust in the love that supports us.

The mother reflects on how she has raised her children. She recalls their joyful greetings each morning. When did wariness creep in, and the absolute trust break down? Suddenly, cries occur not only from distress; there are dark periods of isolation, fear, and competition. To the mother, how deeply she loves her children is beyond question—they are the most wonderful people in the world. The children knew that once, too. So the doctrine of original sin reveals the insight into our common experience of having our freely given gift of love questioned, tested, and even rejected. As any mother will agree, the most painful thing her children can do is not know how deeply they are loved. They push up against the love, test it, mock it, attack it—and we can only wait and hope that the years of holding them, singing to them, and nurturing them have left a message in their bones. Once the loud clamors of adolescence, peer pressure, and identity crisis have quieted down, their being will tell them they have been deeply loved. And having lived through the experience with our children, we might more easily go beyond fear to the knowledge that we are loved.

Chapter 6

Death

Each of the fears present in circumstance, conflict, suffering, and guilt finds its strongest expression in the fear of death. If circumstance is the determining situation beyond our control, death is the circumstance of circumstances. If conflict is the fear that we must leave part of ourselves behind in the choices we make in life, death demands that all be left behind. If suffering is incompleteness, loss, and pain, how much is death an image of suffering. And if guilt is the impossibility of making reparation, death seems to be the seal of guilt, closing off for all time our chance to turn from evil and to do good. We found earlier that in each of the boundary situations, by entering into the fear or by making a choice against it, we could discover a way of being in the world without having a need to flee from the fear. Can that way extend even to overcoming our fear of death?

It is also related that when Rabbi Nahman was at the point of death, Raba entered into a compact with him to reveal the great secret of life and death after he had passed away. Rabbi Nahman kept his word and appeared before him in a dream.

"Did you suffer any anguish?" asked Raba.

The spirit of the dead man answered, "The Angel of Death drew my soul away with as light a hand as one draws a hair out of a jug of milk. Nevertheless, I wish to assure you that, even if the Almighty were to order me back upon earth to live my life all over again, I would refuse because of my fear of death."[1]

The overriding significance of the fear of death colors most philosophical and political systems. This fear can take the form of a denial of any meaning. Existentialism takes the position that there is no meaning to what we do and suffer here because we are destined to surface but briefly on this planet, only to fall back into death. "The final terror of self-consciousness is the knowledge of one's own

71

death, which is the peculiar sentence on man alone in the animal kingdom. . . . Death is man's peculiar and greatest anxiety."[2] People form
political societies to protect themselves from physical death and religious societies to protect themselves from spiritual death. "The dear-
est thing to every animal is its own constitution and its consciousness
thereof."[3] All our lofty aims and ambitions are seen to exist simply to
disguise our terror in the face of death.

The seventeenth and eighteenth centuries saw a breakdown of belief in a conscious, deliberate creation. Along with this declining belief came acceptance of the view, put forth by the philosopher Thomas
Hobbes, that the fear of death is the prime motive in all human action. To be sure, there are people for whom this is not so, but they
are found for the most part in societies in which the system of meaning has not broken down.

Our concern with death is intimately related to our concern with
birth and the broader cosmological concern, "Where do we come
from?" In the twentieth century, the latter question has been largely
reduced to a sexual one, though a full reading of Freud reveals that
the sexual question is itself the religious/cosmological one. We are
witnessing a proliferation of books on death, related to the proliferation of books on sex—sex not as transcendent, but as worldly; not as
pointing to a higher reality, but as restricted to those few pleasures
that humans can bestow on themselves. Our anxiety about death resembles our anxiety about sex in that both betray our incompleteness.
Sex shows us that we are partial—that only in union and communion
with another can we be whole. The problem is negated if we can join
communally with another. Death shows us that we are finite—limited
in relation to the external world. This is problematic only if we feel
we must be infinite in ourselves, rather than by participation in the
infinite. If we must be all things—whole and complete—in ourselves,
we must fail. But if we can recognize that our wholeness and completeness rest not in ourselves but in the larger whole to which we
belong and contribute, we have not failed and need not fear.

Women's insights into death come not from abstract speculation
about death, but from their actual role of caring for the aged and dying.
This care is undertaken not with the objective of conquering death,
but rather with the idea of easing the passage from life. In the course
of caring for the aged and dying, we can become aware of a series of
experiences that are common to those who reflect on their own imminent death or on the death of a loved one. We can begin to perceive
the dying not as alien, terrifying, and radically different creatures—as
our society often does—but as people like ourselves who have needs

and concerns related to our own. Such a realistic approach to the dying has had concrete benefits for terminally ill patients. It can provide great benefits for a new spirituality as well. In reflecting on the experiences of the dying, women in the role of mothers can recognize a process already familiar to them. In the course of aging and of seeing their children mature, they have mourned the loss of an earlier sense of themselves and have found a way to transcend that loss. We will now examine how our participation in the process of dying and mourning can contribute to spirituality.

To enter into the fear of death or to make the choice against this fear, we must first reclaim the dying. As long as we regard death as a misfortune peculiar to the dying rather than an experience common to all, we cannot go beyond fear. Here the work of Elisabeth Kübler-Ross is so important, because she brought the dying into our consciousness and forced us to confront what we most feared.[4] Prior to Kübler-Ross's work, the terminally ill were frequently relegated to back wards, and physicians often denied that any of their patients were dying, at least to the patient if not to themselves.

LANDMARKS IN DYING

The pervasive attitude in the medical establishment has been a concern for control and mastery over sickness and death. It is clear, then, why medicine has found it difficult to deal with death and dying (over which it ultimately has neither control nor mastery). Kübler-Ross concerned herself with understanding and relating. In working with the terminally ill, she identified five stages, which she found were applicable in all cases of significant loss: denial, anger, bargaining, depression, and acceptance. Further research has shown that these stages do indeed occur, and generally in that order, although not necessarily in such a clean, linear progression. In other words, a person can in the course of one day experience stages one, four, three, and one again, in that order. Nevertheless, the five stages remain profoundly valuable as descriptive of human experience and as landmarks that apply in many other areas of our lives. In the course of a life we experience many transformations. We are subject to physical loss (such as loss of vision or loss of our youthful vitality) and emotional loss (death of a loved one, separation from a friend, divorce, and the letting go inherent in child-rearing). From one perspective, we might say that life consists of many little deaths.[5] Since loss or transformation is so central to life, Kübler-Ross's work has direct application to spirituality.

We have defined spirituality as coming into relationship with reality. We cannot achieve a full relationship with reality as long as we are governed by a fear of death. This fear manifests itself in many ways. For example, rather than acknowledge our own mortality, we avert our eyes from the dying; we avoid confronting death by defining the self in terms of mind; much of the hatred directed against the flesh is really displaced fear of death; finally, women, because they are identified with caring for people's *physical* needs, have tended to become substitute targets for this hatred. In our desire to disguise from ourselves our own fear of death, we have chosen to hide the dying, the aged, the sick, and even the women and children—all those in our society who are vulnerable or who are identified with the physical— because they remind us that we ourselves are physical and thereby vulnerable to death.

If we are to come into relationship with *all* of reality, including our bodies and our changes, we must come to terms with death and dying. Evelyn Underhill describes a path to spirituality that is open only to the spiritual elite and is unavailable to those of us living the lesser adventures of ordinary lives. But if coming into relationship with reality is the fulfilling of our human potential, then spirituality is possible for all who are open to the full human experience—the experiences bounded by birth and death.

Underhill, in systematizing the traditional "way" to spirituality, delineates five distinct stages, or landmarks.[6] If we now compare Underhill's five landmarks with those of Kübler-Ross, we will find a surprising correlation between the stages of dying and the traditional mystic stages toward spirituality. Eventually we will also see how the landmarks in dying can be used by everyone, not just the spiritual elite, for achieving spiritual growth.

Kübler-Ross	Underhill
1. Denial	1. Awakening
2. Anger	2. Purgation
3. Bargaining	3. Illumination
4. Depression	4. Dark Night of the Soul
5. Acceptance	5. Unitive Life

Although at first glance the two lists appear unrelated, in fact they correspond quite closely. Kübler-Ross's fifth stage, acceptance, is not mere resignation, it is peace—a moving beyond fear and despair. It is the feeling described by "the patient who always believed in a miracle, who one day greeted us with the words, 'I think this is the miracle—I am ready now and not even afraid any more.'"[7] Such acceptance is close to the state of equilibrium, peaceful joy, and intense certitude described by Underhill as the unitive life.[8] The two fourth stages, dark night of the soul and depression, also point to the same experience. Depression is the letting go of everyone and everything that is necessarily inherent in dying. In the dark night of the soul, there is also the final letting go—that of the human instinct for personal happiness. Our grasping prevents us from experiencing full acceptance or unitive life.

Having noted the similarities between the two lists in stages four and five, let us now examine the apparently disparate experiences of the first three stages. Awakening refers to the process of becoming conscious of divine reality. Denial, while seeming to represent quite the opposite idea, actually presupposes an awakening. We cannot deny what we do not know, nor repress what we have not experienced. Denial comes only with awareness—until we are aware that we are dying, we have no need to deny it. The distance between awakening and denial seems greater than it is.

Purgation is saying "no" to many aspects of the self and its experience. Aware of the infinite and of perfection, the self wants somehow to purge its own finiteness and imperfection. All that separates the self from God must be eliminated by discipline and mortification. Purgation is a landmark of pain and effort. Anger, too, is saying "no." It, too, is a reshaping of the self in terms of the new limits set by dying. It, too, is an experience of pain and effort.

Illumination brings a certain apprehension of the absolute, a sense of the divine presence. It is not union, but it is also a joyous stage. Bargaining is a plea for a little more time—one more outing with the family, a chance to fulfill one more task. It forces us to clarify what is important and what we are willing to sacrifice in order to achieve it. When the bargain succeeds, it too is an occasion for joy. Kübler-Ross's examples of bargains are especially moving. One involves a mother who wants above all to attend her son's wedding. She learns self-hypnosis for pain management and attends the wedding without anyone being able to perceive the real extent of her illness. Another example involves an opera singer who wants to sing one more time before all her teeth are extracted so radiation therapy can begin. Her audience is restricted to other members of her seminar on dying, but it fills her need.

The five spiritual landmarks will be examined later in more detail.

The correspondence between them and the stages encountered by the dying suggest that death should not be denied but explored. In the process, we can gain a deeper understanding of life that can help us achieve a profound, natural spirituality.

VALUES DISCOVERED FROM THE DYING

Kübler-Ross summarizes a major insight she gained from her extensive experience with the dying. "It appears that people who have gone through a life of suffering, hard work, and labor, who have raised their children and been gratified in their work, have shown greater ease in accepting death with peace and dignity compared to those who have been ambitiously controlling their environment, accumulating material goods, and [accumulating] a great number of social relationships but few meaningful interpersonal relationships which would have been available at the end of life."[9] The values revealed in this quotation correspond with those we have been exploring in our search for positive uses of boundary situations. While we are facing or undergoing suffering we wish that it need not be. But those who have not attempted to avoid suffering, but rather have accepted and gone through it, have been able to find some meaning and value in it. Similarly, those who have worked hard and labored have made reparation for life by finding a way to give. In contrast stand those who need to control their environment. If dying (whether to life or to a particular aspect of life) is learning to let go and let be, those who must control their environment will find acceptance of any loss or transformation most difficult. Those who must accumulate, be it objects or people considered as objects, will be thwarted by their very possessiveness. Buddha, with his receiving but nongrasping hand, remains a powerful image to help us go beyond suffering.

FORMS OF SYMBOLIC IMMORTALITY

The acceptance of the dying, of our own mortality, and of the letting go in death is a step in going beyond the fear of death. The next task is to arrive at some meaning that can transcend death—some set of beliefs or values that we deem eternal. Robert J. Lifton describes such values as forms of "symbolic immortality."[10] We will see how these forms make us aware of those lasting values with which women have traditionally been concerned.

Immortality through Offspring

One response to the fear of death has been a quest for personal immortality. The "Epic of Gilgamesh," written in the nineteenth century B.C.E., concerned the search for eternal life. While the desire for personal immortality has continued through the centuries, people since at least biblical times have settled for the more limited aim of immortality through their offspring. Such "biological immortality," while not providing us with eternal life, allows our self to live on symbolically through our biological descendants. The quest for such immortality usually results from a preoccupation with the narrow interest of preserving the self in the face of death—or at least, that portion of the self that is transmitted to descendants—to the extent possible.

Immortality through Humanity

Symbolic immortality through offspring can be viewed in a different light if we regard our self as *giving* life rather than seeking it. Instead of clutching at life, we relax our grip on it and focus on the process of letting it pass through us. The image of Buddha's open, nongrasping hand symbolizes our new concern. Instead of hoarding life for ourselves, we bestow it without fear. In one respect, the difference between seeking life and giving it resembles the difference between our ways of using cisterns and wells. A cistern contains a limited supply of water, so each drop is carefully measured out. A well is filled with the waters of a flowing spring, so the more it is used, the fresher and more plentiful the water.

A natural concomitant to the process of giving life, or allowing it to pass through us, is the ability to expand our concern beyond our own offspring. The experience of mothering provides us with the insight that the biological contribution represents merely the beginning of the parenting process. Beyond it lie years of caring concern that constitute the bulk of the maternal contribution to our offspring. This contribution can be extended to encompass not only our biological offspring or our adoptive descendants, but all members of our community and, finally, all of humanity as well. Allowing our concern to expand enables us to adopt a new form of symbolic immortality, immortality through humanity. If at the same time we can identify our own being as part of the being of all human life, we can more easily accept personal death because we identify with a deathless value—the ongoingness of humanity.

Identification with humanity, embodied in the dictum to love our neighbor as ourselves, has been recommended to us since at least the time of the Hebrew prophets. The problem is less one of wanting to love our neighbor than of being able to do so. The process that can lead the self to a genuine identification with humanity involves a transformation of consciousness. Usually, our consciousness is concerned with knowing rather than relating. We "know" people by those physical characteristics and personal habits that distinguish them from others. Our task is to know them not by what distinguishes them but by what we share with them. That means we must go beyond knowing them by external criteria—from outside them and outside ourselves—to understanding and relating to them from within, through the shared experiences of the human condition. We must also change the manner in which we perceive others. Our knowledge of others is filtered through the Kantian categories of the understanding, including space and time. We must now allow for a concept of time that differs from the customary linear, unidirectional model. In considering a person, we can be aware not only of the present but also of the past and future. To view an active, curious infant is to be conscious of its source. At the same time, to view it as human is also to see its future, even in the present. The curious child we once were lives on within our self alongside the aging grown-up, not just as a memory but as a real force in our life.

The process of breaking free of our usual mode of consciousness allows us to experience the being rather than the passing of time and thereby also the being rather than the passing of human life. The boundaries imposed by time—including the ultimate boundary of death—become less and less significant. Breaking free of our usual mode of consciousness also enables us to relate to and identify with human life because the boundary of self has become less important. Through such identification with humanity we can achieve a symbolic immortality that extends beyond what we can achieve through our offspring.

Immortality through Nature

Our identification with humanity can expand even further to an identification with all of nature. Women have traditionally been associated with nature and the natural, though frequently to their detriment in a society that aspires to the *super*natural. The identification with nature has come about for many reasons. Among these are the comparable cycles of fertility and gestation shared by women and other living things, the apparent similarities between women and nature in transforming a "dead" seed into a living being or plant, and the similarity in the roles played by women and Mother Nature in supporting and sustaining life. Women's sympathetic identification with nature can help transform our view of the world from an alien earth through which we wander to a homeland in which we can be deeply rooted. We can find meaning in the realization that while we come to be and pass away, nature—of which we are a part—goes on. By participating in the immortality of nature, we would conform to the Buddhist ideal of a human being as one "who would wait for all others to enter Nirvana before entering himself, who would be willing to wait 'till the grass is enlightened.' "[11] If we realize that we need not dominate or control nature, we can find in it a value that transcends death.

Immortality through Creating

"One way to reduce the patient's fear of death is to re-arouse his creative impulses."[12] Our abilities to create can foster yet another form of symbolic immortality. Once again the nongrasping hand of Buddha serves as a guiding image. Not through the existence of "permanent" monuments to us, in the form of buildings (let us say) or portraits, is symbolic immortality through creating achieved. Rather, it is found in the act of creation itself, which demands a shift of concern from the self to what the self can contribute to the world. The contribution need not be—indeed cannot be—permanent. By creating, we give of ourselves and in so doing—giving life rather than seeking it—assuage our fear of death.

Creating—as opposed to creation—focuses on the process rather than the product. Overriding concern with a product, an outcome, or a goal results from a linear view of time. Implicit in such a view is a means-ends relationship in which the value of any action is measured by its contribution to the outcome or goal. The linear view of time plays a central role in Western theological systems, which emphasize an end of days, a final judgment, and an afterlife. Contrasting with the linear view of time is the cyclical view, which is rooted in women's tradition both historically and, more important, ideologically. The cyclical view of time emphasizes not the goals of life but its processes—creating, mothering, and letting go. A woman giving birth to a child creates not an end product but a process—an infant that immediately partakes of the process of change. Mothering and letting go are processes that similarly foster another process—life. Through the insight into the experience of women passing on the gift of life, we discover that what is deathless is not a creation but participation in the ongoing process of creating.

IMAGES OF DEATH AND OF LIFE

Beyond the landmarks in dying and the forms of symbolic immortality lie images of death. Lifton offers three images of death: as separation, as disintegration, and as stasis. Looking at the reverse of each of these concepts gives us images of what it is to be alive.

One implication of death as separation has been drawn out in Joanna Macy's work on despair.

> The bomb is one expression of the suicidal tendency of the social habits that derive from our conception of ourselves as separate beings. Once we conceive of ourselves as separate and isolatable, then our drives to compete and get for ourselves a place in the sun are destructive of the very bases of our existence.[13]

If death is viewed as separation, life by implication is connection. The power of this image lies in earliest childhood experience. We exist not as isolated entities but as parts of a child-mother relationship. Separation would indeed be death. Fuller life lies in deeper and richer connections, as exemplified by the Bodhisattva's caring concern extending finally to every blade of grass. Underhill quotes a Sufi statement: "Pilgrimage to the place of the wise is to escape the flame of separation."[14] The flame of separation is that which isolates us and locks us into the narrow confines of self. Wisdom is the empathetic identification that allows us to feel our kinship with all of being.

When death is viewed as disintegration, life is seen as integration. Again, the image of life is founded in earliest childhood experiences, where

> the mother is needed as someone who survives each day, and who can integrate the various feelings, sensations, excitements, angers, griefs, etc. that go to make up an infant's life but which the infant cannot hold. The infant is not yet a unit. The mother is holding the infant, the human being in the making. The mother can, if necessary, go over in her mind all that the day has meant to the infant. She understands. She sees her infant as human at a time when the infant is incapable of feeling integrated.[15]

There was a time before integration, and death appears to us in the image of that time. The need for integration—unity not only of the physical life but also of the spiritual—is stressed by Eckhart: "The many [must be] made one in you. Thus, the more multiplicity there is, the more you will require unity in yourself, if one is to be changed into the other."[16]

Finally, death viewed as stasis implies that life is composed of movement, growth, and change. We see this clearly in the infant's delight in motion and in our own discomfort before an unchanging scene. Change may be unpredictable but it is alive. Stasis is the epitome of deadness.

The three images of life that derive from the views of death bring us back to our definition of spirituality: *coming* (the affirmation of the centrality of process, motion, and change) *into relationship with* (the essential foundation of connectedness) *reality* (that which unites all our experiences into one integrated whole). We can see now that the definition derives from the process of becoming human—a process made conscious for us by the insights of women into mothering.

LOVE

The fear of death causes us to yearn for another world. As we have seen, a familiarity with dying provides one approach to overcoming this fear. Another way to go beyond fear is to discover the factor that is stronger than the fear of death.

> In the last resort we must begin to love in order not to fall ill, and we are bound to fall ill if, in the consequence of frustration, we are unable to love.[17]
>
> All that is living must be loving so as not to die.[18]
>
> Love is fierce as death.[19]

Love is the force that can overcome the fear of death. It allows us to accept vulnerability and loss of control. Love, by shaking up our conceptual scheme, shifts our center of attention and changes the relationship between "I" and "we." The concept of "I" changes as love expands the ego boundaries to include the object of one's love. Love fights the death instinct, which would close us off from our environment. We are able to live, knowing that we are going to die, by loving. Love takes us out of time, where the fear of death is located, and to be outside of time is also to be beyond causality. It is this experience—of being beyond time and causality—that allows people to die for love or for an ideal. On some level they no longer see death as an absolute. So spirituality is a training in love that dispels the fear of circumstance, conflict, guilt, suffering, and even death. Freud makes very clear the tension and threat brought on by openness to the environment. He suggests that we have wrongly conceived of the organs of sense perception—that we use them not so much to open ourselves to our environment as to control what comes to us from the environment.

> The sense organs . . . consist essentially of apparatus for the reception of certain specific effects of stimulation, but . . . also include special arrangements for further protection against excessive amounts of stimulation and for excluding unsuitable kinds of stimuli. It is characteristic of them that they deal only with very small quantities of external stimulation and only take in *samples* of the external world. They may perhaps be compared with feelers which are all the time making tentative advances towards the external world and then drawing back from it.[20]

We long for control, and one way of achieving it is to suppress all diversity. But absolute control is a form of death. We must open ourselves to differences to gain a new perspective so that something genuinely novel can emerge. This way lies threat, but this way, too, lies life.

Freud is committed to the life-giving force of Eros. He advocates that we accept its influence and is fully aware of the pain and suffering that the living frequently endure. That suffering leads Camus to write, "there is but one truly serious philosophical problem, and that is suicide."[21] Camus draws this conclusion from the premise of the absurdity of the world and the pain of being the only center of freedom and meaning in a meaningless world. Freud does not regard the world as absurd, even though he is acutely sensitive to the pain caused by extensive contact with it. He finds that we defend ourselves against pain by a species of suicide, the death instinct, which tries to reduce all our contact with challenge, threat, and stimulation. Love provides the imperative to life, but it is won only through an ongoing struggle against the forces of inertia, defense, dissolution, and insensitivity. Even health itself is won only by overcoming resistances to health, for the healthy organism is alive to its environment.

The ability to choose life is based on an altered evaluation of suffering. The ego defends itself against pain, displeasure, or suffering. The person who can affirm life and accept vulnerability must not deny the reality of suffering but must accept it as essential for personal growth. Freud's *Analysis Terminable and Interminable* opens with an account of a Russian man "spoilt by wealth" in whom Freud is to reawaken the interest in life. Freud succeeds, but only up to a point. He sees that "the patient found his present position *highly comfortable* [italics mine] and had no wish to take any step forward which would bring him nearer to the end of his treatment."[22] He concludes that "in every phase of the patient's recovery we have to fight against his inertia, which is ready to be content with an incomplete solution."[23] So the resistance to health comes about because of a conflict between comfort and tension: we have the desire for an immediate, if incomplete, solution rather than a willingness to undertake the harder, ongoing process. Josiah Royce sees the acceptance of tension, the thwarting of present impulses for the sake of higher unity of experience, as an essential religious commitment.[24] To choose life, tension, and the thwarting of immediate gratification for the sake of higher unity should be our central spiritual stance. A choice against death is the choice of passing on the gift of life. It is the choice that allows children to grow up as independent selves, challenging and extending our perspective. It is a choice made not once, but repeatedly in the ongoing process of mothering. Mothering represents our choice of Eros over Thanatos—love over death.

MOURNING

Women's spiritual contribution does not come to us as rules or theories but as narrative. We learn spirituality through the lives of those who have come before us. Earlier, the story of Leah gave us one model of women's spirituality. Now, as we look at women's responses to the trials of circumstance, conflict, guilt, suffering, and death, we can look to the story of a woman who has somehow faced these negative boundary conditions and, through her response, teaches us something about mourning and comfort. In many respects, Elisheba, wife of Aaron and sister-in-law of Moses and Miriam, experienced in her own life the sudden anguish and reversal of fortune associated with the biblical Job.

There was a woman who came out from Egypt named Elisheba. The woman was blameless and upright, known even in her own lifetime as "a woman of valor"; she feared God and shunned evil. Four sons were born to her, and because she was married to Aaron, her sons were to have the exalted role of serving in the Tabernacle along with their father. The day of the dedication of the Tabernacle arrived:

The happiest of women on this day was Elisheba, daughter of Amminadab, for beside the general rejoicing at the dedication of the sanctuary, five particular joys fell to her lot: her husband, Aaron, was high priest; her brother-in-law, Moses, king; her son, Eleazer, head of the priests; her grandson, Phineas, priest of war; and her brother, Nahshon, prince of his tribe. But how soon was her joy turned to grief! Her two sons, Nadab and Abihu, carried away by the universal rejoicing at the heavenly fire, approached the sanctuary with censers in their hands, to increase God's love for Israel through this act of sacrifice, but paid with their lives for this offering. From the Holy of Holies issued two flames of fire, as thin as threads, then parted into four, and two each pierced the nostrils of Nadab and Abihu whose souls were burnt, although no external injury was visible. [25]

This story, recounted in the Midrash—the collection of stories that rose up around the biblical tales to fill in the gaps—ends at this point. It is left for us to imagine how the comforters of Elisheba differed from those who actually discomforted Job.

A messenger came to Elisheba's tent and said, "Your husband and four sons were serving in the Tabernacle when a fire came forth from the Holy of Holies and killed Nadab and Abihu. Your cousins have carried their bodies outside the camp. But Aaron, being the high priest, may not take part in the burial." Then Elisheba arose, tore her robe, cut off her hair, and threw herself on the ground. And Elisheba cursed the day on which she was born and said, "What mother should live to bury her sons?" When the women heard about the deaths they each came from their tents to console and comfort her. They sat with her on the ground seven days and seven nights. None spoke a word to her for they saw how very great was her suffering.

The women maintained their silence. They knew all too well what their husbands were saying. There was not a tent in which the events at the dedication of the Tabernacle were not being discussed, but they never brought their husbands' arguments into the tent. Elisheba was free to say all that was burning within her without contradiction from them. On the seventh day, the prophet Miriam suggested that the women go out, and she took upon herself the task of leading Elisheba out of her tent to the edge of the camp and then returned her to the people. While Miriam returned Elisheba to the community, there remained a sense of Elisheba's remaining "outside the camp" in her mourning.

Part of being Elisheba is seeing an aspect of reality that other people are at pains to disguise. We really don't want to know how much suffering there is and how vulnerable to it we are. But Elisheba, in mourning, knows it first-hand. She can no longer accept glib assurances. She is "outside the camp" seeing the fragility and—to some extent—artificiality of the camp. The usual goals of life no longer attract her.

People loved and revered Aaron for stoically accepting God's judgment on his sons and felt disquiet with Elisheba's untempered grief. Some of the women accepted the negative assessment of Elisheba, but most did not. They understood her need to mourn, to feel outrage, to resent Aaron's withdrawal from her and refusal to express anger.

We have Hannah's prayer for children because she prayed in the presence of a man. But Elisheba's prayer after the death of her children is one of the great unrecorded prayers. It was not a prayer of petition—her sons were already dead. She knew she couldn't change the past and she didn't know there was anything she could want. Nor was her prayer one of confession, thanksgiving, or intercession. She just wanted God to know all that was in her heart. She gave us a model of prayer as staying in conscious relationship with God. Her prayer was an expression of her anger at God and at what life had dealt her and a trust that God could hear the anger and stay present.

Elisheba's losses eventually helped her to love. Initially they estranged her from Aaron and from much of the community. Elisheba's two other sons, Eleazer and Ithamar, grew distant as if they didn't want to "catch" whatever had wiped out their brothers.

After Nadab and Abihu died, people began to say evil things about them. It was bad enough to say evil things about the living, but to say them about the dead was to compound the wrong. The dead could not defend themselves. They all had known Nadab and Abihu and knew they were not evil. But people had persisted in saying they had offered alien fire, or they had drunk wine before entering the inner court, or they had not hidden their faces when God spoke to them on the mountain.

Elisheba felt fury rise within her. "You have not learned the lesson of the manna. Has the righteous person gathered more than the unrighteous? Has God not given to each just as much as each person needs? The manna does not prove your righteousness or unrighteousness and Nadab and Abihu's deaths do not prove their evil or goodness."

Nadab and Abihu died, but we don't know why. We do know that we mustn't be trapped into blaming the victim or turning away from those in pain. The lesson of the manna did not prevent later religious teachers from looking for someone to blame in times of disaster. They could not accept that everything is a gift and that prosperity is not an indicator of either merit or blame. They kept asking for justice as if love were something you could justify. "Why do you love me?" is the wrong question. "How do you love me?" comes closer.

"How should I respond to your loving me?" closer still. "Please help me to respond fully to your love" comes closest. God showed Elisheba this love, not by preventing the death of her children or accounting for her children's deaths, but by abiding presence, concern, and attention. God remained present through her silence and withdrawal, through her angry cries and accusations, and through all that followed. The deaths of Elisheba's sons were not a punishment, and they are no more explained than are any children's deaths. But Elisheba was able to love God. She did not know what death might mean, but she came, over a long process, to trust.

In Elisheba's mourning we see a woman able to introduce and transmit her own experience of a compassionate God. Like Elisheba, we don't "get over it"; we grow around it and somehow a space is left— a space for God's presence. We cannot give healing to others. We need to wait and let them come to their own insight. We know that in every desert there is or can be revelation. We do not know how healing takes place, and we don't have to know. We just need to be authentic, let the process take place, and allow time and space for all that is in the heart to come out. We don't want to be like Bildad who, in responding to Job's suffering, said: "How can a man be just before God,/ One born of woman be clean?" We cannot imagine the comforters of Elisheba saying any such thing.

They said nothing at all. They were silent because their task was to listen, to be fully present to the one who was in mourning. They knew you cannot give another your wisdom, only your presence. They didn't have to drown out the disturbing things that Elisheba said. They understood that "why me?" is another way of crying, that they should not take it as a literal statement. They prepared food, and they sat. They cleaned up and sat. And they never silenced Elisheba but allowed her to express all that was in her heart.

So we learn from Elisheba's story the importance of presence, of silence, of time and mystery. We learn that just because we don't have the answers doesn't mean that God has none. We learn not to blame but to love. And we learn how phenomenal humans are. We know that Elisheba's love for her other children was not a reward for her having suffered but an indication of her reengagement with life.

Healing

We need to wait, to be patient—which means to be open, receptive, and noncontrolling. That is hardest to do when we most want to "fix" something. Fixing is usually not an option, but love is, and patience is, as are openness, honesty, and presence.

According to a rabbinic tradition, God creates the world anew daily, something we cannot believe when we are in mourning. We cannot imagine anything new ever happening that could transform the way we feel. And rationally, nothing can: another child, after all, is not a replacement for the lost child, another love does not replace the lost love. What makes creation new is not the existence of other children or other loves but the opportunity we are given to re-create—and thereby heal—ourselves. If we don't change, the presence of others to love is irrelevant because we are not open to them. We discover that there are others to love *because* we are healed, not as a means of healing. So by newly creating the world, God makes healing possible. God enters into the emptiness of our loss, accepts our rage, our confusion, our pain, and slowly, organically, shapes us to grow in a new way.

People shape us by inspiring our love, and they shape us by giving us cause to mourn their loss. Eventually we must part from all those we love: either they die or we do. We are shaped both by their presence and their absence. We are shaped so that we can love better.

As a mother, Elisheba must have bemoaned all she had failed to do for Nadab and Abihu. Her comforters, if they truly offered solace, didn't rush in to reassure her but recognized and respected the natural sense of inadequacy we feel when confronted with the death of one we loved. Our love may be infinite, but we have only a finite time in which to express it. We feel fear and loss, but we also feel guilty, in part because we have survived. The dead can suddenly take on an air of sanctity: they were better than we are, we should have died instead. And when the death is out of order—the children preceding the parents—the guilt is intense.

The process of mourning is crucial to healing. Without it we may not only lose components of comfort, such as reminiscences and presence, we may also lose some of our present aliveness. The past is part of the present, and we build on it. Our past is always changing, but we lose its gifts if we repress it. We can choose to enter the desert of mourning to reclaim gifts lost to repression.

The women seated around Elisheba may have done sewing or weaving as they sat around her—their repeated motions comforting her. There was no need to explain. Often Elisheba didn't address them, but she was never unaware of their presence. Their presence made it safe to explore the terror of her own feelings and doubts.

What happened to Elisheba and Aaron's marriage? It became clear to Elisheba that her covenants were inextricably intertwined. She could not be angry with Aaron without being angry with God, and she could not rage against God without feeling fury at Aaron. A complete healing would have to include both. When Elisheba could finally forgive herself for having been unable to protect her sons, she could forgive Aaron. He might have been able to forestall plague, but, like her, could not protect Nadab and Abihu.

She knew that people mourned in different ways and at different speeds. Aaron had been denied the opportunity to bury his sons and to assist physically in the process because of his role as priest. He was also the leader of the Tabernacle worship and so he could not in public give full vent to his own feelings. Initially, that had been estranging for Elisheba. He could not enter into her expressions of hurt and rage. He even attempted to quiet her. Over time, she came to understand and forgive his own incomplete mourning.

We have witnessed in our own families people who have mourned completely and people who have deadened themselves and refused to explore all the aspects of their grief. In either case it is the comforter's task to be present but not to determine the rate or extent of the mourning process.

Through her mourning Elisheba experienced revelation and recovered the authentic voice she had long put aside in her ordinary life. From studying her mourning we learn: No one ever died to teach someone a lesson. Each of our lives is of ultimate significance. Our lives and deaths are related to ourselves and to God, they are not props for someone else's drama. So Nadab and Abihu's deaths were not to punish Aaron for the Golden Calf, to test him, or to test Elisheba. Aaron and Elisheba turned this tragedy into a kind of test by their attempt to stay in relationship with God through the greatest pain of their lives. But they knew that Nadab and Abihu had an identity and value beyond just being their children. They, like each one of us, were precious in God's sight, and their life and death concerned God.

We have looked at the positive uses of negative boundary conditions. But loss remains loss, so we have also explored mourning and how women teach us how to enter fully into this process and emerge with deeper integrity and compassion.

Chapter 7

Love, Unity, Joy, Contribution, and Birth

As we have seen, the boundary situations focused on in traditional spirituality—circumstance, conflict, suffering, guilt, and especially death—have provided us with occasions to flee this world. But we have also seen that viewing them with the insights women offer provides opportunities to explore the world more deeply.

Only when we have faced the meaning of death can we become free to live. "A free man thinks of nothing less than of death, and his wisdom is not a meditation upon death but upon life."[1] Yet we should be aware of the extreme one-sided nature of these boundary situations. Certainly, part of what it is to be human is to confront them, but if we define what it is to be human only in negative ways, we estrange ourselves from some of our most important experiences. We must discover and recognize the value of positive boundary situations as well.

Our study of women's intimate role in caring for the dying contributes to spirituality by allowing us to have a deeper understanding of death, which is one of our primary spiritual concerns. But women stand at the border not only of death but of birth. They find within their own experiences not only suffering but joy. They are aware of circumstance as a spiritual concern, but they can use circumstance to discover love. They know conflict, but they also know unity. And they suffer guilt, but they find within guilt the seeds of contribution. We now have before us an entirely new set of boundary situations that provide us with a *positive* view on the major spiritual concerns. They represent women's contribution toward a more complete vision of spirituality.

"Pray at times of dejection and at times of exhilaration."[2] What it means to pray "is to pay attention to something or someone other than oneself. . . . Choice of attention—to pay attention to *this* and ignore *that*—is to the inner life what choice of action is to the outer."[3] Attention, in traditional spirituality, has focused on our times of dejection. We must now complement the picture and add the times of exhilaration to our view of the human condition. Joy is as real as pain and just as worthy of serious consideration, if we are to know ourselves fully and to understand how we fit into the rest of reality.

LOVE

Examining the boundary situations from a negative view leads us to a positive view, which must be made part of a full spirituality. In exploring the first of the situations, circumstance, we find that pushing beyond the initial terror reveals that while we cannot sustain ourselves, we are nevertheless sustained. This awareness leads us to conclude that we are loved, so circumstance may be said to point to love. If until now we have focused our attention on circumstance, we must now explore the positive boundary situation of love. However positively we may regard it, though, love is neither easy nor untroubling. Perhaps "perfect love casts out fear"[4] but, paradoxically, our greatest fear may be the fear of love.

The fears inherent in circumstance recur in love. Just as circumstance proves love, love proves circumstance. The description of circumstance as consisting of those factors beyond willful control is the description of love as well. Love cannot be controlled, which is why it must be a gift. "Everything can be taken away from us except love, and this is what makes love unique and something we can give."[5] Love cannot be wrested from us; it is closer to us than our physical bodies, which can be taken; it comes closest to who we are. It is frightening to have something that is so essential to us outside of our control.

The love that we receive is the same as the love that we give. The gift of being loved is also the gift of being free to love, though we cannot be compelled to do so. We can hoard the love that surrounds us. Withholding our love damages those who could be nourished by it and damages us as well. We may fear loving because we fear vulnerability. The person we love may cause us pain by changing, by dying, or by rejecting our love. We long for some way of loving that can nourish and sustain those we love without depleting us. We seek a kind of loving that would be an action (something we choose) rather than a passion (something we experience willingly or not). That there exists such a love, one that is not suffering but that transforms suffering, is one of the insights that can come through spirituality.

Love's Responses to Otherworldliness

In the face of fear, we are tempted to flee to another world. As we saw earlier, the other world is really a new relationship to the things of this world. "There ought to be . . . some way of loving that can go with a sense of the otherworld."[6] The love that shows us that this world *is* the other world can be found in the scriptures of many religions. In Buddhism this position is expounded in the metaphor of a ferryboat, representing Buddhist doctrine, crossing the rushing river of becoming and change (*samsara*) to the distant bank of liberation. From the shore of spiritual ignorance we cannot see or even imagine the shore of enlightenment, or liberation. It takes an act of faith to step off the shore onto the ferryboat of Buddhism. After a while we lose sight of our former home, but the shore of liberation is not yet visible. This is a frightening time, and we endure it by focusing on the boat itself (the doctrines, rituals, and disciplines of Buddhism) until finally the shore is reached.

> When such a one turns around to look again at the land left behind, what does he see? What *can* one see who has crossed the horizon beyond which there is no duality? He looks—and there *is* no "other shore"; there is no torrential separating river; there is no raft; there is no ferryman; there can have been no crossing of the nonexistent stream. The whole scene of the two banks and the river between is simply gone. There can be no such thing for the enlightened eye and mind, because to see or think of anything as something "other" (a distant reality, different from one's own being) would mean that full Enlightenment had not yet been attained. . . . Illumination means that the delusory distinction between the two shores of a worldly and a transcendental existence no longer holds.[7]

A passage from Genesis describing the second day of creation expresses a theme that can be related to the Buddhist story:

> God said, "Let there be an expanse in the midst of the water, that it may separate water from water." God made the expanse, and it separated the water which was below the expanse from the water which was above the expanse. And it was so. God called the expanse Sky.[8]

The significance of this passage lies in God's separating the preexisting waters rather than creating distinct water for the heavens, so that the waters above are the same as the waters below. What is in heaven is of the same substance as what is on earth.

In Buddhism the way to cross from ignorance to enlightenment is through compassion. In the Jewish and Christian traditions the way to go beyond the illusion of two opposing worlds is the same: "He may be reached and held close by means of love, but by means of thought never."[9] Here "he" refers to God, but the idea that God is accessible through love, not analytic thought, suggests that in a world that we love, we experience neither the absence of God nor estrangement from God, but envision the world as having its being in God. Love is so natural to us, is indeed our birthright, how then do we come to distort and lose it? We begin in a state of innocence, that is, lack of awareness. We are completely dependent on love, but are unaware of the dependency. Our first knowledge of the love that supports us brings on an awareness that the love can be withdrawn. Wisdom initially produces fear—fear of vulnerability, pain, and death that obscure the love that could transform our world—but wisdom when perfected gives rise to loving desire.[10] We must not turn aside from our fear but go forth to meet it.

Definition of Love

To see why withholding love damages us and how love can transform our world, it is necessary to clarify what we mean by love. Spinoza, who sees love as the way beyond suffering, defines love as "joy with the accompanying idea of an external cause," joy being the movement from a lesser to a greater perfection.[11] An entire view of reality is captured in that definition, and the more we examine it the more we discover. For Spinoza, love is not reduced to the level of feelings. The courtly love that restricts the world to the beloved's glance or approving smile does not qualify as love, but only as a form of narcissistic indulgence. To love is also to grow, and to withhold love is to be locked in the isolation of the self.

Women's experience in mothering can provide us with an insight into the meaning of love. Spinoza writes that the love of God toward us and the intellectual love of the mind toward God are one and the same.[12] In other words, the gift of love (God's love for us) is our capacity to love. While we may know that, we keep forgetting it, but we can look to women's experience to remind us. Mothers love their infants, and that love just flows and flows. One day the unresponsive bit of life smiles back. What a triumph! A mother could try to remain in that dyadic relationship, loving her child and being loved by it, but such a life would be stifling to both. Mothers love their children so that, secure in the love they receive, the children are enabled to love others—to pass on the gift of love and life. Our ability to love is proof that we have been deeply loved.

Mothering and Love

"The mighty revelations to which the religions appeal are like in being with the quiet revelations that are to be found everywhere and at all times."[13] Mothering is an ideal process in which to look for these quiet revelations. It recalls to memory our earliest longings, which recur in transmuted forms in adulthood. By reflecting on mothering, we learn that love is ever-changing. We speak about constancy in love, yet our earliest experience is of a love that is adjusted to the needs of the beloved: the love of the needy infant is all-absorbing, while the love for the growing toddler is supportive but less intrusive.

Love is not a possession to be hoarded up; if it were, it could be measured and found diminished or increased. Rather, it is a liberating process to be transmitted, and its form changes as we become increasingly able to give love ourselves. When we are finally able to transmit fully the gift of love, we find that our capability to do so has largely resulted from our mother's love for us.

Reflecting thus on mother love enables us to understand Spinoza's assertion that God's love for us *is* our capacity to love. The title "God" has been used to refer to widely divergent experiences. Theologians are in agreement that we cannot define God, that to define is to limit. Nevertheless, the title evokes images in the minds of most people who hear it pronounced. In an attempt to break through those largely unexamined images, Spinoza interchanges the words God, Nature, and Substance. For the same reason, I suggest that we substitute for the question "What is God?" the question "Where is God?" Our attention is then shifted to those situations in which we have experienced reality and value. If we locate God as being in and through all our experiences and beyond what we can hope to experience, we find the thought of God to be conducive to openness and expansiveness. This idea of reality, as something progressively revealed to us throughout our experiences and ultimately inexhaustible, is what I mean by God.

To regard this reality (God), rather than our self, as the source of our love radically influences our view of love. If we believe *ourselves* to be the source of love, then we tend to believe that the love (a) is under our control, (b) reflects our own potentialities and abilities (and can be no greater than we are), and (c) can be judged on the basis of the satisfaction it provides us. But if the love comes from God and we are only the conduit, then it is not under our control, it is greater than we are and can therefore transform us, and it cannot be measured.

It is a paradox that we can attempt to focus on only one of the images of God to the exclusion of the rest of reality. In the process, we lose God.

> At midnight the would-be ascetic announced: "This is the time to give up my home and seek for God. Ah, who has held me so long in delusion here?"
>
> God whispered, "I," but the ears of the man were stopped.
>
> With a baby asleep at her breast lay his wife, peacefully sleeping on one side of the bed. The man said, "Who are ye that have fooled me so long?"
>
> The voice said again, "They are God," but he heard it not.
>
> The baby cried out in its dream, nestling close to its mother. God commanded, "Stop, fool, leave not thy home," but still he heard not.
>
> God sighed and complained, "Why does my servant wander to seek me, forsaking me?"[14]

Finally, we need to know how we should love. Eckhart writes, "I am to love my friend for his own sake, for the goodness and virtue of him, for all that he himself is and then I shall truly love him, in the only real sense of the word."[15] When has our love been not for the sake of our own welfare but because of the goodness of the other's nature? Once again women in their role of mothering offer significant insights. In bearing and raising children, mothers provide us with a model and with the most common instance of true love.

UNITY

Conflict, we saw, occurs within ourselves as a sense of division, within our relationship with others as an experience of discord, and with reality as a basic experience of a hostile environment. We can identify a boundary situation of unity that complements the vision of the human condition defined by conflict. Unity in the individual appears as single-pointedness, simplicity, or wholeness.

Wholeness

We spend much of our time torn between the conflicting demands of our self, others, our rational expectations, and our emotional desires. Division is familiar to us but so is wholeness. Our experiences of single-pointedness or simplicity, when they occur, are the best evidence that wholeness is not merely the absence of division or conflict, but a powerful force in its own right. For example, when an athlete runs a long-distance race, there may come a point where nothing exists but the next step. Earlier there had been the hope of winning, the determination to run with a particular strategy, the attention to competitors, and the consciousness of the crowds. But over the course of the race, everything but the next step drops away. In time multiplicity will crowd in again, but that moment, when every aspect of the self is focused on the next step, seems to point to something beyond itself—an experience that the runner once knew and aspires to know again. Such intense focusing can occur not only during moments of extreme physical exertion, but also at times of extreme emotional trial. At times of crisis, despair, great joy, deep realization of love—the extraneous and the irrelevant just drop away. The intense experience eases and multiplicity comes rushing in, but in reflecting back on that time, we realize that part of its meaning for us was the wholeness of the self involved in the experience. Can these fleeting moments become waymarkers for a whole life? Can we live our lives so that everything feeds the single unifying principle?

The experience of single-pointedness in an extreme physical or emotional state, though it may recur, is transitory. It is a fleeting glimpse or vision of possibilities, but given the extremes under which it occurs, it provides an unlikely model for a way of life. Yet other situations through which we live engender the same single-pointedness over a long period of time. During pregnancy many women experience a change in the direction of their interest. Winnicott notes that the woman "slowly but surely comes to believe that the center of the world is in her own body. . . . As you become more and more sure that you will soon become a mother you begin to put all your eggs into one basket, as the saying is. You begin to take the risk of allowing yourself to be concerned with one object, the little boy or girl human being that will be born."[16] Winnicott's discussion of this experience felt by some women during pregnancy is important in two respects: (a) the "putting all your eggs into one basket," as he calls it, or single-pointedness as I have been describing it, occurs over a period of many months—it is not a fleeting occurrence but a prolonged experience; (b) we become alert to the risk involved in single-pointedness.

If we have all had *moments* of wholeness, simplicity, or single-pointedness, and yet our basic experience is one of division and conflict, something must be restraining us from single-pointedness. The cause of this restraint is fear. Notwithstanding images of the serene Madonna (images found not only in paintings but mirrored in the faces of our pregnant relatives and friends), we fear single-pointedness. We believe that a single-pointed life must be somehow distorted or unbalanced and must leave out important human experiences. While this fear may apply in most areas of human endeavor, in the spiritual domain we find at last something we can love with all our heart, all our soul, and all our might, as Deuteronomy 6:5 exhorts us.

Accord

We all have had moments where the otherness of other people startles and dismays us. We wonder what reality must be like if different people can perceive it in such opposed ways. But we have also had moments of deep accord with others—moments that are in their own way just as challenging to our view of reality. We must ask how it is that people can sometimes understand each other so well. Heraclitus writes that the waking have a single cosmos in common, but in sleep each turns away from the common cosmos to something that belongs to that person alone.[17]

Freud extended the cosmos—the world we hold in common—to encompass our dreams as well. Freud's landmark study, *The Interpretation of Dreams,* "opened to our understanding not just the meaning of dreams but also the nature and power of the unconscious."[18] More important here, however, is the autobiographical nature of the work and the implication that Freud can contribute to *our* understanding through *his* autobiography. If Freud's interpretation of his own dreams can be of value to others, it can be so only because something of him is within each of us. We all want to be able to share and to be understood at the deepest levels, yet we fear the prospect as well. The tension between the "I" and the "we" persists. There must be a type of accord, harmony, or coming together that preserves the uniqueness, individuality, and value of the separate parts.

Peace

Peace is the sense of being at one with reality. It may occur in the absence of war or in the quietness of nonconflict, but it can also occur within the fury of struggle. Peace as achieved by Buddha leads him to say, "Sure is my release."[19] If release is peace, then that which keeps us from achieving peace is confinement, constriction, or holding on. To be in conflict with reality is to be shut up against it, to grasp, to clutch, and to be unwilling to let go. Paying attention to our breathing gives us an analogy to the larger peace to which Buddha points. If we hold our breath, the very process of holding it becomes painful as our lungs become constricted. Before we can breathe again we must let go—and that letting go, that release, brings a feeling of relief. Breathing is essential for survival, but even though we need breath we cannot store it. We must trust reality sufficiently to let go of it and then to await its return. If we can extend our area of trust, then the release, the joy, and the peace that Buddha experienced is ours as well.

Women and Unity

Wholeness, accord, and peace are aspects of the same phenomenon, unity, viewed first within the self, then with other people, and finally in relation to reality as a whole. In our example, wholeness grows out of women's experience during the nine months of pregnancy. Within this experience lies an instance not only of internal wholeness, but of accord and peace as well. The developing fetus may be totally dependent on the mother, but it remains distinct from the mother. As we noted earlier, its cycles of sleep and wakefulness are frequently at odds with the mother's. Yet this otherness is accepted and accommodated. The wonder that someone distinct from us can be so closely connected finds its extreme example in the mother-fetus relationship. This relationship helps us see lesser connections all around us, uniting separate beings in acceptance and accommodation.

Peace is our sense of oneness with reality. It too finds expression in the mother's experience during pregnancy. The mother cannot know or control the myriad factors that are essential for the healthy development of her child. The time of pregnancy can be one of terror, as we try to foresee all that can go wrong. But more often it is a time of peace—a letting go of our need to control, in the trust that reality will support this growing life.

In pregnancy, then, women gain the experiences from which they can extract wholeness, accord, and peace, which comprise the positive boundary situation of unity.

JOY

Spinoza contends that "we suffer in so far as we are a part of Nature," but joy can overcome that suffering: "The greater the joy with which we are affected, the greater the perfection to which we pass, and consequently the more do we participate in the divine nature."[20] Joy is the expansion of the self, the movement from a lesser to a greater perfection. It should not be confused with pleasure, which operates on the level of feeling and as such is subject to a counter-feeling. Pain can negate pleasure, but it cannot negate joy. In fact, pain suffered for the sake of growth or for something we care about is consistent with great joy. For example, pain accompanying the stretching exercises of a ballet dancer or an athlete can increase joy. Still, we are sometimes faced with intense pain that seems to be meaningless. But if we *can* find meaning in and through our pain, we can then accept the pain for the sake of our growth.

Locating joy on a level deeper than feeling does not mean that joy is merely a theoretical construct. We do experience joy: we experience it as expansive. Joy does not bring a cessation of pain; rather, it transforms our relationship to the pain. But changing our relationship to the pain actually transforms the experience. If we feel pain (from physical or emotional causes), our first impulse is to try to ease the pain. But if we knew that the pain held an important insight for us, we would cease to *suffer* it and actively attend to it. If we knew that the pain was transforming us, we would still feel it, but now we could give some meaning to our experience.

If suffering is the constriction and isolation of our self—that which drives the self back in on itself—then joy is the expansion and going out of our self and the expansion of our area of concern. The greatest joy, then, should be compassion, a point Buddha makes in the Parable of the Mustard Seed. In the story, a woman's only son has died. In grief she asks all her neighbors for medicine to revive him. The neighbors respond that the child is dead. One man, however, responds that while he cannot supply medicine, he knows a physician who can and directs her to Buddha. Buddha answers her request by asking for a handful of mustard seed to be taken from a house where no one had lost a child, husband, parent, or friend. The woman goes from house to house but finds none in which a beloved person had not died. She comes to realize that her grief is selfish.[21]

The Parable of the Mustard Seed gives us two examples of joy. By analyzing it, we can see what women, in their role as mothers, can teach us about joy. The story begins with a mother's grief on the death of her only son. At some time prior to his death, her sense of self had expanded to include her son—he had enlarged her world. While this expansion may indeed bring joy, it is also frightening. The expanded world does not belong to the mother fully but is mediated by the son, who is mortal. When he dies, her world once again becomes constricted. At this point, Buddha's cure is introduced. She must again expand her sense of self, but this time not in a mediated fashion—by, let us say, having another child—but by loving others as she had loved her son. Death is common to all but joy is to surrender selfishness.

Dunne makes the same point in answering the question "Who enjoys bliss in the midst of suffering?" with "Blessed are the compassionate."[22] Spinoza comes to the same insight as he struggles with his own sorrow. A certain kind of knowing, an intuitive understanding, the kind of prelinguistic, preanalytic knowing that a mother has of her infant, the knowing that is empathetic identification, brings joy to the mind. In using this kind of knowing, Spinoza perceives accord: "Those things which are connected with others—as all things that exist in Nature—will be understood by the mind, and their subjective essences will maintain the same mutual relations as their objective realities."[23] This vision of compassion and accord leads to the most liberating experience, love. Saint Theodoros sees the end of all practice as love: "From such practice grows the precious flower of dispassion. The offspring of dispassion is love, which is the fulfillment of all the commandments binding and holding them in unity."[24]

CONTRIBUTION

Guilt, as we saw earlier, arises naturally in the life process. The same life process also affords occasions for reparation, which is a remedy for guilt. But not all our impulses of giving, creating, or contributing arise out of repentance; we may, for example, give out of fullness. Contribution out of fullness constitutes one of the positive boundary situations that women in their mothering role can bring to a full spirituality. Mothering exemplifies contribution in passing on the gifts of life, of love, and of care, that had earlier flowed into the mother. Out of fullness and abundance, women give to their infants the love essential for the infants' growth.

When our contribution is motivated not by a need to assuage guilt but by fullness, our contributing is joyous. The experience of contributing out of abundance rather than deficiency is one of exuberance and excess of energy. It resembles the feeling of vitality that we associate with running up stairs out of sheer energy and delight in our strength, and the experience of singing as we perform some task, not because our song is required but because of our abundance. When our action, performance, or creation has its source in fullness, it may be demanding, but it is experienced as unstrained.

The situation of contribution is especially instructive because it lies in the area that unites the "I" and the "we." We contribute because we are part of something larger than our own lives and efforts, but the form of our contribution is based on our uniqueness and our individuality.

> Every person born into this world represents something new, something that never existed before, something original and unique. "It is the duty of every person in Israel to know and consider that he is unique in the world in his particular character and that there has never been anyone like him in the world, for if there had been someone like him, there would have been no need for him to be in the world."[25]

The Psalmist exhorts us to "sing a new song." The boundary situation of contribution is the domain of our freedom in which we can shape a new song out of our experience and insights, keeping before us the example of the mother contributing to her infant joyously out of her fullness.

BIRTH

If death is the boundary situation that brings into stark relief the fears implicit in circumstance, conflict, suffering, and guilt, then birth stands parallel to it, forcing us to think through the fearful but essential aspects of love, accord, joy, and contribution. The fear of love, implicit in the fear of birth, is so overwhelming that we frequently experience it in its parts rather than its whole. We fear that the infant may not be born whole. Then we fear that we haven't the skill to care for it. We fear the many dangers the child must navigate before it reaches adulthood. Behind all these fears is the awesome realization that our happiness is inextricably connected with the being and well-being of the child. Not for one month or eighteen years, but for the rest of our lives, our child's fortune will color our own. To allow someone to touch us so deeply requires trust and courage, and that is precisely what is at stake in love—not just mother-child love, but all love.

Birth, which is in some ways a paradigm of accord, is also a paradigm of conflict. If our children are to be fully alive and free, the day will come on which they will rise up and proclaim their otherness. We sense the otherness from the earliest days when we cannot understand their crying, or when food is pushed away. But the challenge to our perception and our values comes later, and it is rarely experienced without pain. We always meant for our children to belong to themselves; we may know that letting go assuages the pain and eases the conflict; but it is hard to let go of those whose fortunes are so inextricably connected to our own. The joy inherent in birth is accepted with consent to the pain inherent in birth. We consent to letting another's life touch us at the deepest core of our being, forever. We consent to letting the process of raising the child transform us as it forms the child.

Eckhart writes that "the supreme purpose of God is birth."[26] Although Eckhart is referring to the birth of the son of God in the soul, let us consider the statement literally. The end (purpose) of life then is not death, but more life. The experience of birth is paradigmatically the experience of ecstasy—we are literally outside of our self; it is the experience of an overflowing abundance of love; it is accord with everything that supports and sustains this tiny life; and it is joy—the expansion of the self to cover and hold this yet-unformed self. Traditional spirituality requires us to hold the image of our death ever before our mind. How different might our response to this world be if, instead, we held an image of our birth before our mind. Buber quotes the saying "In the mother's body man knows the universe, in birth he forgets it."[27] Our deepest and most profound yearnings are for a connection, imperfectly imaged, perhaps, in that primal connection we had in the womb. Birth is an invitation not to return to the womb, but to join in love, accord, and joy with the whole; to contribute, out of fullness, by bringing into the world a new life.

Through the experiences of women and reflection on these experiences, we arrive at a set of positive boundary situations that contribute to a new spirituality. We have seen that the exemplary instance of love is mother love; that a prolonged instance of unity is found during the nine months of pregnancy; that joy finds expression in the mother's expansion of the self to include concern for her child; that contribution is exemplified by procreating; and that birth answers death by responding to the fears inherent in circumstance, conflict, suffering, and grief with the trust inherent in love, unity, joy, and contribution.

Chapter 8

Beyond Solitude to Compassion

In the fourth century A.D. the deserts of Egypt, Palestine, Arabia and Persia were peopled by a race of men who have left behind them a strange reputation. They were the first Christian hermits, who abandoned the cities of the pagan world to live in solitude. Why did they do this? The reasons were many and various, but they can all be summed up in one word as the quest for "salvation." . . . In those days men had become keenly conscious of the strictly individual character of "salvation." Society—which meant pagan society, limited by the horizons and prospects of life "in this world"—was regarded by them as a shipwreck from which each single individual man had to swim for his life.[1]

Thus begins what is to become the model for the spiritual life. Even adherents to this model who are to stay "in this world" turn inward to work out their solitary salvation. Solitude and loneliness become earmarks of the spiritual life as traditionally constructed. There is an initial plausibility and attractiveness to this model that is worth examining. We are more than what other people do to us, more than the social roles in which we are cast, as we learned so cogently in Hagar's story. In light of that, the quest for solitude can be seen as a systematic stripping away of what society has foisted on us, in order to discover our essential self. The solitary quest for that essential self is based on a common experience. We find ourselves in contexts in which we feel divided against our self and estranged from our true values. We are convinced that if only we could shed those parts of our self that are not truly us, we would be authentic once again. But stripping away the aspects of self foisted on us by society in order to discover our essential core may prove as futile as stripping away the skins of an onion to arrive at the essential core that we assume is there. What of our experience of being divided against ourselves by a society whose values we oppose; doesn't the very fact that we can have such an experience demonstrate the existence of an essential self independent of society? This seeming paradox is resolved when we realize that society is not monolithic. We may negate one society by going off to the desert, but that still leaves us with the society that we affirm by choosing the model of the Desert Fathers. The sense of self we reject by leaving the pagan world does not leave us with an undefined sense of self. Rather, it leaves us with a sense of self defined within a theistic world view.

THE DESERT EXPERIENCE

Women's desert experience differs from that of the male Christian hermits in three important ways, as we will see if we use Hagar's sojourn as a model. First, unlike the Desert Fathers, Hagar does not choose the desert but is forced into it. There is a critical difference between seeking aloneness and accepting aloneness. The former is the way of negation, a rejection of society. The latter is the way of finding meaning in whatever life thrusts upon us. Our life unfolds in such a way that from time to time, will it or not, we have our desert experiences. They are marked by radical aloneness, when the structures that normally support us are removed and all we can depend on seems to come from within. Second, Hagar neither fights against her experience nor submits to despair. Rather, she accepts her situation and begins to look within herself for the strength to endure it.

The third way in which Hagar's experience differs from that of the Desert Fathers is that she doesn't stay in the desert. Sent there involuntarily, she has a profound vision and then returns to the world. The value of the desert experience lies in the transformation that it can bring about in the self—a self that must pass on the gift through action and interaction in the world.

A contemporary example of a desert experience might be found in a hospital on the night before a woman is to undergo a radical mastectomy. After the last visitor has departed, the woman is offered a sedative but decides not to take it. She does not distract herself by watching television or reading a novel. Instead she looks ahead: the next day bodes pain, a change in her body and her body image, and possibly even death. In those hours before surgery she is in the desert, not because she chooses to be and not because she rejects the rest of the world. She is there by virtue of the circumstance, and it forces her to look within to find what can nourish and support her even then. After surgery, she will return to the world, to her family and her friends, transformed through what she has learned about herself and anxious to pass on this gift.

THE SENSE OF RESPONSIBILITY

What makes the idea of the solitary struggle so plausible is not merely our awareness of conflict with the larger society around us. In part, the solitary struggle derives its appeal from our sense of responsibility. If we are to be saved, then we ought to be doing something. We are responsible for the way in which we live our lives. No one can become enlightened for us; it is our solitary task. This view conforms to our experience of taking responsibility, but that's not the whole story. Much of who we are and what we become depends not only on what we do, but on the people who are sent to us and the people to whom we are committed. Part of what it is for Leah to be Leah is to have been the sister of Rachel, to have struggled a lifetime to win the love of Jacob, and to have raised Reuben, Simeon, Levi, and her other children. Can anyone argue that she would have been the same person, achieving the same spiritual awareness, had she had no sister, been unmarried, or remained childless?

Somehow, within our own being, we must balance the two claims on us of responsibility and relationship. To choose one, as traditional spirituality has done, at the expense of the other is to formulate a spirituality that is inadequate to the needs of a full humanity.

SOLITUDE

Solitude attracts us as a trial and a discipline—we regard the ability to be alone as an achievement. What we fail to acknowledge, however, is that it is not *our* achievement but that of a nurturing mother who gave us the ability.[2] The capacity to be alone and to enjoy and profit from solitude *is* an achievement and also an important sign of emotional maturity. The most significant factor in the development of this capacity is the experience of being alone, as an infant and as a young child, in the presence of one's mother. "Thus the basis of the capacity to be alone is a paradox; it is the experience of being alone while someone else is present."[3] At stake in the capacity to be alone is a relationship of the individual to an internal object that "provides of itself a sufficiency of living, so that temporarily he or she is able to rest contented even in the absence of external objects and stimuli."[4] The infant, with a weak ego organization, can be alone because the mother provides reliable ego support. Gradually, the ego-supportive environment is internalized and becomes part of the personality of the individual. Then, and only then, does the capacity to be alone arise, and even then one could say that the individual is not really alone. In our deepest aloneness we find present within us the mother who cared for us in infancy.

LONELINESS

Along with the capacity for solitude, another powerful human experience lends credibility to the notion of the solitary struggle: the experience of loneliness. Loneliness does not necessarily occur whenever we are alone, nor is the experience restricted to those who are alone. Loneliness can occur in crowds as well as in solitude. And yet the two concepts, loneliness and solitude, are intimately associated. If happy solitude implies the ability to rest contented in the absence of external objects and stimuli, then loneliness implies an inability to rest contented in their absence and, perhaps, a closing off from them even in their presence. To the lonely person, the objects and stimuli either are not present or cannot be experienced. Something within that person is creating separation and distance. Loneliness, then, has to do with a discomfort with ourselves coming from an inability to touch and be touched by others. Solitude may exacerbate loneliness, but it may also be an important step toward healing it. In considering boundary situations, we saw that the way through them necessitated first that we fully experience them, whether it was the terror implicit in circumstance or the pain involved in suffering. For loneliness to be healed, it must be felt and faced. Distracting ourselves does not cure the essential discomfort within and actually makes it harder to recognize and confront the discomfort. In other words, solitude, rather than causing loneliness, provides a valuable approach toward understanding it. Loneliness presents us with a barrage of symptoms, each of which must be experienced and worked through to arrive at the peace, the rest, or the sufficiency of internal living that marks the capacity to be alone. The process unfolds as

> despair, fear, anxiety and self-rejection to the emergence of a new strength that fights for control, reason, perspective and a faith that

is adequate to meet all there is of life, its pain and delight, its lone-liness and fractured relationships as well as its joy and supporting rela-tionships.[5]

From this perspective, solitude is seen as having something to do with wholeness. However, it is also seen to be neither a goal in itself nor a way to reject society. Solitude must be taken as an occasion to explore the discomfort with ourselves and the impediments that block our relationship with others.

SELF AS ISOLATE

Behind the notion of the solitary struggle for salvation is the assump-tion that the self is an isolate and, further, that salvation is individual. The notion of the self as isolate can be maintained only by discount-ing our birth, our nurturance, our education, and our continued suste-nance. Even the view that the human species is isolated from other species can be discredited as we become aware of all that nour-ishes and sustains us. In fact, even the human as individual lies open to question. Mitochondria, which differ in genetic makeup from hu-mans, nevertheless comprise a large proportion of human bulk. Lewis Thomas writes of them: "There they are, moving about in my cyto-plasm, breathing for my own flesh, but strangers. They are much less closely related to me than to each other and to the free-living bac-teria out under the hill."[6] When we speak of an individual, then, we are actually referring to a conglomerate.

The view of the self as isolate is due to an inability on our part to acknowledge our dependence. We begin, in infancy, in a state of de-pendence so total that we are not even aware of the mothering that supports us. But while still in infancy, we move from absolute depen-dence to relative dependence as we become aware of what nourishes and sustains us. As we move toward independence, what is achieved is not self-sufficiency or isolation, but growth in our ability to recog-nize the mothering we have received. We come to understand what has been given and to recall it so as to nourish the inner life. We realize that we are never independent of our need for food, warmth, and the oxygen that sustains life. A recognition of our dependence is a form of independence.

The belief that salvation comes through relationship is supported by many great spiritual teachers. Whatever view they may have held before the start of their spiritual lives, their later insight encompassed love, compassion, interconnectedness, and interdependence:

Pilgrimage to the place of the wise, is to escape the flame of separation.[7]

All real living is meeting.[8]

No one is a saint alone, only self-righteous.[9]

Nothing . . . is more useful to man than man.[10]

Spinoza envisions a world in which the minds and bodies of all
should form, as it were, one mind and one body, striving together to
preserve their being and together seeking their common good.

SELF AS SOCIAL

To recognize that we are not involved in a solitary struggle for individual salvation is not yet to discern what our connectedness might
mean. The task, then, is to try to see how life in union and communion with others is like or unlike the life of the Desert Fathers.
Neither the solitary hermit nor the person living in the world is
really alone. Both are nourished, supported, and sustained by other
people and by other beings. To a large extent what distinguishes hermits from persons in society is their awareness—or "conceptual images of things"[11]—that defines the domain of value. Things simply are;
our awareness conceives and labels them as good or evil. Spinoza systematically develops the significance of this awareness. First, he defines idea:

> By idea I understand a conception of the mind which the mind
> forms because it is a thinking thing. *Explanation.* I use the word "con-
> ception" rather than "perception" because the name perception seems
> to indicate that the mind is passive in its relation to the object. But the
> word conception seems to express the action of the mind.[12]

So the way we conceive of the world is through a mental action. It
is, in fact, the ground of all our other actions and therefore forms the
basis of all ethics and spirituality. We do not passively perceive the
world, we actively conceive it, and our mental concepts constitute
the domain of value. Spinoza, in agreement with the sixth-century
Saint Maximos the Confessor, asserts that whatever has positive being
is good. Something termed "evil" is evil not in itself but in the way
we conceive it and subsequently use it. "By reality and perfection I
understand the same thing."[13] Spinoza then draws out the implication of the role played by our mental concepts in a world that is essentially good.

"Love is joy [passage from a lesser to a greater perfection] with the idea of an external cause." Applying Spinoza's definition, we see that both the hermit and the person living in this world reside in a world that is essentially good. Both are preserved in their being and well-being by other people and other beings. The hermit has chosen to be unaware of that, while the person in this world is aware. But to be aware that our being and well-being come as gifts from others is to love others, if love is "joy with the idea of an external cause." So the significant difference between the person who consciously and deliberately flees the world and the person who consciously and deliberately lives in this world in union and communion with others is a difference of love. When Lewis Thomas reflects on the mitochondria in his cytoplasm, he moves from the startling awareness that he is not an isolate to a positive realization.

> They feel like strangers, but the thought comes that the same creatures, precisely the same, are out there in the cells of sea gulls, and whales, and dune grass, and seaweed, and hermit crabs, and further inland in the leaves of the beech in my back yard, and in the family of skunks beneath the back fence, and even in that fly on the window. Through them, I am connected; I have close relatives, once removed, all over the place.[14]

What starts out as loss of one's individuality ends up as a celebration of relatedness.

Thomas's vision comes close to that of the Bodhisattva, whose kinship and caring concern for being extended to single blades of grass. Our greatest difficulties, perhaps unfortunately, do not arise from relationships with blades of grass or mitochondria. When we examine relationships between people, we discover the difficulties and pains that tempt them to flee into the desert, as well as the value of these relationships. Spinoza concludes that nothing is more valuable to people than people. Socrates, many centuries earlier, suggests the same thing in explaining why he never left crowded Athens for the beauty of the countryside:

> Phaedrus: Anyone would take you, as you say, for a stranger being shown the country by a guide instead of a native—never leaving town to cross the frontier nor even, I believe, so much as setting foot outside the walls.

> Socrates: You must forgive me, dear friend; I'm a lover of learning, and trees and open country won't teach me anything, whereas men in the town do.[15]

We learn from other people. The process can be joyous and rewarding as we feel our undeveloped potentialities flourish in the presence
of others. In a story that illustrates this point, Rosemarie Harding tells
of a woman living in Central America who used to hold a weekly
open-house tea. Each week an Indian woman would come, sit quietly,
and utter a phrase in her native language, which the hostess did not
understand. After a few such visits the hostess memorized the phrase
and had it translated. The Indian woman had been saying, "Thank you.
I will come again. I like who I am when I'm with you."[16] We have
all had that experience of discovering ourselves, our strengths, or our
beauty, in the presence of someone who can really see us. "It was as
if, in his presence, one became more himself. This is the sign of a
holy man."[17]

Learning from other people is not always joyous—it can bring rejection, disapproval, and pain. These possibilities, however, do not
negate its value. Some of our most painful interactions wear away our
protective surface until finally we are truly open. This state of being
truly open is the goal of most ascetic disciplines. It may also be
achieved by fully living in community. Spirituality—coming into relationship with reality—demands openness to reality. Achieving this
openness requires not only honesty but non-defensiveness. Reality is
larger than our conception of it. It has the capacity to transform our
consciousness, but only if we are open to it. If we flee from a major
aspect of reality and carefully structure our experiences so that nothing can challenge our narrow conception of reality, we rule out the
possibility of reality transforming our consciousness. If we separate
ourselves from other people, their many perspectives can neither add
to our view nor challenge and correct it. The process of coming into
relationship with another person tempers our spirit. It is a time of
wonder—discovering who we are in the presence of the other and
discovering who the other person is. It is also a time of fear—longing
to be known but feeling that we are vulnerable. This experience is of
such great value that even the Desert Fathers advise a newcomer to
the desert to put himself under the direction of a spiritual father. The
very same men who praise solitude recognize the potential insights
and spiritual growth inherent in interpersonal relationships. The long
discussion of rules to which the beginner must adhere in entering into
relationship with the father suggests that even more than the father's
experience, the relationship itself is of value:

> When you have taken up your dwelling with a spiritual father and find
> that he helps you, let no one separate you from his love and from living

with him. Do not judge him in any respect, do not revile him even though he censures or strikes you, do not listen to someone who slanders him to you, do not side with anyone who criticizes him.[18]

The Trappist monk and author Thomas Merton writes extensively of his longing for solitude. At the end of his life he is finally permitted to live in a hermitage attached to his monastery. A careful reading of his journals suggests, however, that his deepest spiritual growth occurs not in solitude but during his tenure as Master of Scholastics (students at the monastery). In this role Merton receives the monks for private spiritual direction, confers with them on the interior life, and watches over their development as they prepare for solemn vows and ordination. His caring concern for others is responsible for a major transformation in himself.[19]

The relationship between the Desert Father and the novice or between the Master of Scholastics and the younger monks is modeled on the relationship inherent in mothering. Just as the spiritual father must ultimately step aside as the novice becomes adept, so the mother must step aside as her child develops the strength to live out of its own center. When we finally achieve the capacity to be alone, we must not rest in solitude but must return to pass on the gift to other selves whose loneliness needs healing.

SEEK PEACE IN YOUR OWN PLACE

Loneliness must be treated first by healing the division within the self, then by healing the division between self and others, and finally, by coming into relationship with reality.[20] The healing of loneliness by solitude—by returning to a substitute for the relationship that fostered the capacity to be alone—finds its ultimate expression not in solitude but in compassion, love, and the capacity to meet others in their own isolation. No one wishes to face the terrifying isolation of life-threatening illness. Writer Doris Schwerin nevertheless uses the circumstances surrounding her mastectomy to rethink and reshape her relationship to herself, her relationship to her dead parents, and the situation of her life.[21] She can proclaim, after going through this painful process, that never before has she been so whole. Her healing begins when she identifies with a family of pigeons building a nest on a window ledge across the way. As she watches the family dynamic of the pigeons, she is brought back into active engagement with her own life and with the process of compassionate understanding that eventually heals her. Time and time again we are brought back to the same images: the Parable of the Mustard Seed, the image of the Bodhisattva, our kinship through identical mitochondria—but now we recognize that loving other people, blades of grass, or a pigeon family is a gift not to them but to ourselves. Spinoza's insight that God's love for us is our capacity to love begins to be less abstract. The love that heals isolation and estrangement from others and that gives life can be seen as the gift of love.

Chapter 9

The Spiritual Walk

When we think of a journey, we think of an undertaking that has some length, that requires preparation, that has various stages or landmarks along the way, and always, that has a clearly defined destination. A journey is a journey to some place. The notion of a journey lies beyond the notion of linear time, which is fundamental to traditional spirituality. The various stages along the way acquire value insofar as they contribute to the goal, which lies at the journey's end.

Our concept of the journey is modeled on the journey of the Israelites out of Egypt and across the Sinai wilderness to the Promised Land. That journey is instructive for the spiritual life because we too have been enslaved—to our own egotism and narcissism, to external standards, and to unrealistic goals. But the journey of the Israelites is instructive in another sense. They could not define their progress in terms of miles traveled. Their route was circuitous and frequently circled back over places already passed. In fact, the journey to the Promised Land was not measured in distance traveled but in character transformed. If we could think of our own spiritual way without measuring our progress against some external yardstick or by comparing it with someone else's way, then the journey model can be useful.

In contrast to the journey, we should consider the walk. The length is indeterminate, the walk begins anytime, no preparation is called for, the way is not clearly defined, and we have little concern with distance traveled or landmarks passed because we have no clearly defined destination. In other words, on the journey we are moving *toward* something while on the walk we are strolling *with* someone. The goal of the journey lies at its end. The goal of the walk lies in a way of living and relating, doing and being. It is not some peak moment, after which we live out the remainder of our days in decline, nor is it the end of our days, as we survey our past on our deathbed. The goal is

113

the actual living in day-to-day relationship and commitment. If the walk is a walk with God, then we find that we sometimes draw closer and sometimes draw back in what amounts to a cosmic dance. We approach, we move away, we open up, we withdraw. We turn away but then turn back to see if the beloved is still there. We carry God within us but are startled to find God outside of ourselves—unexpectedly free, real, and not the product of our imagination.

A walk is an undertaking of movement, but at any moment we are precisely where we should be. The walk is taken for its own sake, so because we are not focused on a distant goal, we can notice and enjoy our immediate surroundings and savor the companionship of other strollers without comparing our own walk with theirs. The walk contrasts with the journey in the same way that cyclical time contrasts with linear time. In the domain of cyclical time, as in the walk, value lies not in any end but in the process of life itself.

THE JOURNEY METAPHOR

Traditional spirituality has employed the metaphor of the journey. The journey has been named the inward journey or the journey of the soul to God. The journey to spirituality is, as we might expect, a lengthy undertaking (frequently lifelong); it requires preparation (usually in the form of spiritual direction); and it has various stages or landmarks along the way. Because there is a clearly defined destination, spiritual adepts have mapped the journey.

The journey metaphor has a powerful intuitive appeal. Because we aren't *as* we should be, it is easy to confound that feeling with the notion that we aren't *where* we should be. Also, the motion and change inherent in a journey seem true to our experience. Finally, the idea of a destination seems vaguely reassuring.

But serious problems arise with the journey metaphor. Accepting it means reintroducing, as a central concept of the spiritual life, the Kantian categories we have taken such pains to remove. It is easy to fall back into space, time, number, cause, and effect. We begin to think that part of our life has value only insofar as it contributes to our achieving the destination. And what about this destination? If the spiritual journey is the journey of the mind to God, is God found only at the end of life? Where is God in childhood, in friendship, "where two or three are gathered in my name"? The notion of stages along a journey is so pervasive that it occurs not only in spiritual writing but in writings on developmental psychology, the stages of moral development, and the "seasons" of people's lives, for example.[1] In whatever domain the stages occur, they carry with them inherent traps: comparison and judgment (and the pitfall of spiritual or moral pride); despondency (we are not as "far along" as we "ought" to be); inauthenticity (after stage three we "ought" to be in stage four, and so we misperceive and misname our own experiences). We might also be tempted to hurry someone along because the stages are not intrinsically valuable, but are valuable only insofar as they point to the goal. The Desert Fathers, aware of the dangers inherent in the model of stages of spiritual development, issued a warning that is all-too-often ignored: "It is wrong to seek prematurely, with much speculation, that which comes in its own time and, thereby rejecting what is in hand, to dream of something else."[2] We will explore some of the ideas that have adhered to the traditional formulations of the spiritual journey: the notion of the journey up the mountain, the journey into the desert, and the descent into hell and back. Then we will contrast the journey metaphor with our new metaphor of the walk. Using the non-goal-oriented notion of the walk, we can still find value in the traditional spiritual stages once we regard them as experiences that we may, but need not, pass through as we come into relationship with reality. They will be seen as ways of naming or signifying experiences that occur and *recur.* It would be comforting to believe, as the mystics did, that we need to pass through the "dark night of the soul" only once. That unfortunately does not conform to everyone's experience—the insight gained today must often be rewon tomorrow. Nevertheless, valuable insights remain for us in the five stages of the spiritual way, once we free them from a linear formulation.

Ascending the Mountain

Two things happen when we ascend a mountain: we progress farther away from our usual environment, and we approach our goal. Both these aspects of the ascent are important if we are to understand the differences between traditional spirituality and a new spirituality informed by women's insights. The farther up we climb, the more distant we become from our world. After a while, the normal features of our world take on the appearance of children's toys. The people, their houses, and their enterprises seem diminished, even trivial. It is ironic that to ascend the spiritual mountain, instead of increasing the climbers' compassion and concern, tends in the opposite direction to reduce their normal world to unreality. And what is the goal at the spiritual mountain's summit? It is not an indwelling reality but a transcendent Deity, removed and distant from the world. The process of the climb is difficult and painful—a form of discipline or trial. The goal is the summit; from it the climbers descend again, if they must, only out of compassion to tell those in the valley (or cave) of the light at the top of the mountain.

Our own experience of mountain climbing differs in some important respects from the mystic ascent. First, we stand in a significant relationship to the mountain. We do not simply wish to "conquer" it, that is, to get to the top (by helicopter if necessary); we want to know it. As our foot seeks a toehold, we dare not eye the summit. Our full attention and concentration are given to this rocky ledge, to that low-standing bush growing to the side, and to the loose dirt that slips off the rock we are trying to grab. This ledge is real—it is not final, but here and now it demands and deserves our total engagement. This act of taking seriously every step along the way makes the ascent of the real mountain much more compatible with women's spiritual experience than the mystics' ascent of the metaphorical mountain.

In real life, we do not climb alone. From earliest childhood we have been taught that hikers go off in the company of others because even a minor accident, such as a twisted ankle, can become life-threatening if no one is nearby to help. Sometimes our fellow climbers precede us. They may climb silently, caught up in the demands and concentrations of the climb. Sometimes they warn of loose rocks or point out a sight we may have missed. Occasionally they wait for us and we sit, unhurried, glad to be where we are at that moment. Sometimes we go on ahead, and in rare instances the way broadens, allowing us to continue side by side. Here again, the real experiences of climbing resonate with women's spiritual experience of being aware of the relationships that support them and to which they contribute.

Once we have reached the summit of our real mountain, surveyed the panorama, and rested, we climb down again—not to a cave or to an infested pit but to the beautiful countryside we viewed from the top. This experience is analogous to that of Hagar, who returns to her environment with new inner strength and with increased appreciation for her world. On the way down we meet climbers coming up, and we tell them how much longer they have to travel. Just as on the climb up, we must pay attention to each step because we are more tired now and, although gravity is seemingly on our side, our muscles strain to keep us from hurtling down the slope. The climb down is quieter than the climb up. We can't afford to be lost in memories of the summit. Here and now we must be fully present to the loose rock or the unexpected root. When we reach the bottom, we are back where we began. Now we can reflect on our experience, but more likely we are content to relax and enjoy the warmth and comfort of being home again. The meaning of the climb does not lie in attaining the summit; the meaning is not even in the return. The meaning is, and was, in every step, and in that we have the most important aspect in which women's experience coincides with reality and informs the new spirituality.

The Desert Journey and Hell

The mystic journey into the desert has much in common with the mystic ascent of the mountain. Both entail a negation of what is left behind. The desert journey, like the ascent, is a discipline or trial that is chosen over the comforts and temptations of civilization. The rise of civilization is viewed as a turning from God, so its rejection is thought to reverse that turn. In the desert, stripped of agricultural and technological advances, the mystics are forced to recognize their utter dependence on God.

The desert has a fearsome beauty that is startling to people accustomed to more moderate conditions. Going off into the desert need not be a negation of one's world; it can be a continuation of all that we know about our world. Our survival in civilization is due to observation, familiarity, and awareness of what lies around us. If we are to survive in the desert, it will not be by negating what we have learned but by applying it to a new setting. Here too we must observe, gain familiarity, and become aware of the life in the desert. Birds learn to adapt to the fierce temperature changes by choosing insulated sites for their nests. A tree grows downward until its roots reach a water vein deep underground. Only when its supply of water is located does the tree begin to grow upward.[3] A close examination of life up the mountain or in the desert shows that it does not distance us from our world; it engages us in the world more deeply.

Some spiritual journeys require a descent "to hell and back." The journey to the underworld differs from both the ascent of the mountain and the journey to the desert. It does not imply rejection of this world—that is, we don't flee from here in order to reside in the underworld. Rather, the descent and the subsequent return transform our experience in this world. While both the ascent of the mountain and the journey to the desert are metaphorical journeys, our understanding of these concepts is aided by our past experiences of climbing real mountains and traversing real deserts. The journey to hell is also a metaphorical one, but the reality that might further our understanding of this idea is not so apparent. On closer examination, however, we recognize that hell is the name we give to what we do not know, are not aware of, wish to avoid, refuse to face, and fear. In other words, hell resides in our unconscious, and the journey to hell is the extending of the light of our awareness.

Central to the notions of both desert and hell is a view of radical otherness. Traditional spirituality is based on a pronounced dualism, which finds expression in almost every aspect of life: this world *versus* the otherworld, the profane *versus* the sacred, civilization *versus* the desert, heaven *versus* hell. At the pinnacle of dualism we find male *versus* female. Women's spiritual insights have found these dualistic concepts to be false to their experience. Rather than seeing, for example, civilization and the desert in opposition to one another, their approach to understanding the desert consists of extending to the desert those insights that they obtained by living in civilization. They attempt to understand the unconscious not in opposition to consciousness, but by extending the light of consciousness to a new domain. Inherent in the journey metaphor is a commitment to opposition that negates women's central insight into spirituality: coming into *relationship* with reality.

Experience as a Challenge to the Journey Metaphor

The most serious objection to the journey metaphor as a way to spirituality is that it simply does not conform to our experience. Were we to accept the journey metaphor, then part of our life would be reduced to serving as a means to an end (the final goal of union and communion with God). While it is true that in order to become forty years old we must first reach twenty and later thirty, the meaning and value of the intervening years do not lie in their serving as way stations along the route to forty—that is not how we experience our life. The year we have now is not a way station to anywhere, it is where we live. We do, of course, spend some of the present looking back, and we spend some time in anticipation of the future. But for the most part, this is where we live, and here and now we must find meaning and value. To focus on a time past or a time yet to come is to miss the only time in which we can act.

The spiritual journey fails to accord with our experience in another respect. We do not travel on a straightforward, linear path. The insight we gained yesterday may not be with us today. Even someone steeped in Catholic spirituality finds it hard to recount her life in a linear way. Dorothy Day, a convert to Catholicism and founder of the Catholic Worker Movement, left us an honest autobiography, *The Long Loneliness.* She is convinced that she must follow a straight path from dissolution to conversion to a deepening relationship with God. But in writing her account, she admits to moments of closeness to reality—occasions of true unselfish love with her family, times of delight in the world—*before* she became a Christian. Moreover, she suffers moments of real fatigue, doubt, and even despair, *after* her conversion. To her credit, Day refuses to distort her experience to make it conform to her model. We must be similarly open to our own experiences.

THE MYSTIC STAGES REINTERPRETED

Evelyn Underhill studied the experiences of European mystics from the early Christian era to the death of Blake. In seeking a common thread among the differing accounts, she was able to identify five stages in the mystic journey: awakening, purgation, illumination, dark night of the soul, and unitive life. Even if we reject the journey metaphor, we can find value in the experiences represented by these five landmarks. We have seen that stages in death and dying described by Kübler-Ross offer profound insights once their linear, progressive structure has been discarded. Similarly, Underhill's five stages point to powerful experiences that many of us share.

"The mighty revelations to which the religions appeal are like in being with the quiet revelations that are to be found everywhere and at all times."[4] When we understand what is important about the five experiences Underhill describes, we can reclaim the terms for our own experiences, giving value and dignity to our daily struggles.

Awakening

The awakening is usually preceded by a long period of time in which the self is divided. The spiritual pain is at first dull, a sort of malaise, a sense that what we had thought was important is really meaningless. Because the pain is not constant, the self is tempted to disguise the intimations of a deeper unhappiness. It chooses distraction, diversion, or pleasure seeking. Our deception may hold off the transformation for a time, but finally the anguish can no longer be denied. The awakening is usually marked by an event that, while it may seem precipitous, actually concludes a long process of transformation. Plato's Allegory of the Cave presents a typical description of an awakening.[5] Plato likens our condition to that of a man living with others in a dark cave, chained since birth by the leg and neck so that he can see only the wall of the cave. Behind him burns a fire, and images of things that pass in front of the fire are cast onto the wall. All he sees are the shadows—he has no other vision of reality. Chained as he is, his knowledge even of himself is restricted to the self, whose shadow appears on the wall. If he is released and forced to turn his head to the source of light, the movement and the light are painful. He is at first perplexed by the strange objects before his eyes and is fearful of this new perspective. But if he is led up out of the cave and carefully guided, then after the initial radiance ceases to overpower him he grows accustomed to the objects in the upper world. He then recalls his fellow prisoners in the cave and remembers what passed for wisdom there. Stricken with compassion, he returns to the cave—as confused now by darkness as he initially was by light—and is subjected to ridicule by those still in the cave. If he tries to free them and lead them out, they might well set upon him and try to kill him.

The steps that lead to awakening are carefully outlined. First there is our condition of enslavement. The chains that bind us may result from our own limited perspective, our overpowering emotions, or the values of our society. Then comes our conversion, or turning to the light. We may be freed by the personal inspiration of a significant other or by a sense of emptiness, which may suggest that what passes for reality cannot be all there is. Finally, we experience a radiance, corresponding to the ecstatic experience described earlier. The experience challenges our entire conceptual scheme and terrifies us. As we come to understand the cave, we realize that it is nothing other than the world into which we are born. Our world, when we are newborn, is defined by our needs for self-preservation and survival. It is wholly constricted to that which feeds the self. Awakening signifies an awareness of how confining this perspective is. Something or someone makes us see that there is a reality larger than that defined by our needs. The self is dethroned as it comes into contact with a reality larger than itself. Meaning is now determined not by the self but by something larger that can, in fact, transform the self.

Once we realize that awakening is "unselfing," we see that it is something not reserved solely for mystics. Most of us have had instances when we recognize that something—a person, a moral stand— is more important than we are. These moments are rarely dignified by the term "awakening," and that is unfortunate. Perhaps if we applied that term, we would give the experience the serious attention it deserves.

We all begin as self-protective. Our self, our life, and our values must be preserved. Then the boundaries of the self are changed, and love is a frequent catalyst for this change. When our love is caught up in a great cause, in a calling, or in a person with whom we might share our life, self-protection seems too petty a value. When we view an infant who is the incarnation of our love, that life seems even more important than our own. Dorothy Day writes of Saint Catherine of Genoa, "For the first time she saw and knew the Love in which life is bathed."[6] This statement would describe, no less accurately, most mothers when they first hold their newborn children. Underhill sees awakening as a one-time event—we are asleep to certain values, and then we become forever awake. Our experience, however, suggests that we are forever in danger of dozing off as wonder fades with familiarity. Reading the Book of Numbers gives us an opportunity to contemplate this danger. The chieftains of the twelve tribes bring their dedication offerings for the altar of the Tabernacle. The first chieftain presents his offering:

> One silver bowl weighing 130 shekels and one silver basin of 70 shekels by the sanctuary weight, both filled with choice flour with oil mixed in, for a meal offering; one gold ladle of 10 shekels, filled with incense; one bull of the herd, one ram, and one lamb in its first year, for a burnt offering; one goat for a sin offering; and for his sacrifice of well-being: two oxen, five rams, five he-goats, and five yearling lambs.[7]

The offering is splendid, even awesome. And then the text is repeated eleven times, once for each tribe. As we read, tedium sets in, and our eyes begin to skim the page despite our valiant attempts to keep our attention focused on the subject. In all relationships—between mother and child, between lovers—there is a time that is new when the participants are fully immersed in each other, paying attention to every detail and marveling at the wonder of it all. Then, it often happens that the rituals instituted with relationships begin to grow stale. Is it possible to adhere to customs, fall into routines, and keep repeating rituals over and over without destroying the original wonder? It is, if we forcibly pay attention, remember the revelation of the first days, and keep rediscovering the love in and through the ritual, even when the ritual chafes. How this was done in biblical times is suggested by another passage in Numbers. When the wonder of being suddenly freed from the yoke of slavery in Egypt abated, the Children of Israel considered their misfortunes and complained bitterly. "The Lord heard and was incensed: a fire of the Lord broke out against them, ravaging the outskirts of the camp."[8] In other words, terror was employed to remind the people how it felt to be frightened. When what is old fails to delight us, its value may be remembered only when we fear its loss. Whether through the fire among us or the sudden illness of one we love, terror forces us to recapture wonder. But terror, for all its effectiveness, is not the best way to keep the wonder and insight from fading during the years of familiarity. A better process of strengthening our awareness is purgation.

PURGATION

When we think of the word "purgation," images of fasting, ascetic practices, and long vigils come to mind. Certain extreme practices of the saints color our perception of purgation. Yet what is essential to purgation is not some extreme practice, but rather character formation. The self that has been awakened must now be strengthened. All that obstructs our new awareness must be stripped away, and all that emerges from this awareness must be strengthened. Richard of Saint Victor writes that "the essence of purgation . . . is self-simplification."[9] When the self has found something to love with all its heart, soul, and might, it must not be distracted. The day-to-day trials must not dissipate the energy of the united self. We must strip away all that stands in the way of our relationship to reality: such goals as fame, wealth, and status; fears of failure, ridicule, or isolation; and such habits as irresponsibility, laziness, and forgetfulness. The actual practices of purgation are not important and may even strike us as bizarre. But let us, for a moment, take seriously the analogy of awakening and dozing. We have surely all had occasions when dozing was something we dared not do, whether we were listening to a lecture, reading late at night, or driving while very tired. Our intention is to stay awake, but gradually the lecturer's voice fades, the text on the page blurs, or the road hum lulls us into letting our eyelids drop. Suddenly, we are struck by fear. For a few minutes, the rush of adrenalin caused by the fear of lapsed attention keeps us awake. But then once again, sleep lures us. We do anything we can think of to stay awake: dig our nails into our hands, throw ice water on our face, slap ourselves on the cheeks. The only consideration is that we stay awake—sleep would be dangerous.

Let us return to our earlier example of wonder—that of the mother who is euphoric at the birth of her child. Where nothing had existed before there is suddenly a living being to whom she is intensely connected. But getting up for midnight feedings, cleaning an infant who spits up just after being changed, and spending hours comforting a crying, colicky infant all take their toll. She tires, and the danger arises of losing the vision of "the Love in which life is bathed."

A practice that will keep her—and us—awake is found in the rituals of relatedness. Saint Theodoros declares that "from such practice grows the precious flower of dispassion. The offspring of dispassion is love, which is the fulfillment of all the commandments binding and holding them in unity."[10] The practice is not usually referred to as purgation, although applying the term might strengthen our resolution and animate us in our daily efforts. In the mother-child relationship, the practice consists in the daily tasks of child care: feeding, diapering, bathing, playing games, and tucking the child into bed. The practice is not love, but it creates the environment that nurtures love. Practice or rituals of relatedness occur in friendship as well. "Without the letters of condolence, telegrams of congratulations and even occasional postcards, the friendship of a separated friend is not a social reality. It has no existence without the rites of friendship."[11] The practice expresses and later sustains the reality of love.

In a different context, if we awaken to religion, we keep its commandments. This keeping of the commandments expresses our awakening and sustains it but, more important, serves to transform the self so that what we once viewed as a commandment, we now see as the deepest expression of our own desire. When we first discover a friendship, we do things to help or please the other person because that's what friends do. In the process, we gradually come to do these things because we want to do them. The daily caring for our child at first expresses our gratitude and wonder. Later, it sustains and strengthens this wonder. Finally, the practice transforms us so that our caring becomes an expression of our being.

Purgation is not a one-time discipline but a way of life. It transforms our consciousness so that tasks once done out of duty are now done out of love, naturally and joyously springing from our transformed nature.

Illumination

The transformation that occurs through a life shaped by discipline frees us to see the world in all its wonder. Underhill, writing about the soul, describes this experience of "illumination": "She opened her eyes upon a world still natural, but no longer illusory."[12] Insight is no longer restricted to the momentary peak experiences. In all our actions, we are aware of an ease, a joyousness, and a rightness of what we do. Formerly the self was divided between the call of the wonder perceived in the awakening and the demands of prudence, anxiety, and social custom. Now the self is unified and aligns itself with the wonder. Our actual physical perception seems brighter and clearer, as if we had suddenly removed a set of fogged glasses through which we had been viewing the world. Instead of seeing the world constrained by our needs and fears, we now see it without obstruction. Tasks seem easier because illumination, rather than distracting us from our work, makes our performance more efficient. Illumination gives us not a vision of another world, but a new vision of this real—and valuable—world.

Unlike awakening, illumination is a prolonged state, though not a permanent one. Indeed, it is hard to understand how we can feel so joyous, so natural, and so at peace, and then be assailed once again by doubts and despair. Our experience bears out that we do, periodically, become unified around some center. This unification may require a struggle, but once achieved, it is followed by a period of peace. Then the peace gives way to another struggle, which Underhill, following Saint John of the Cross, terms "the dark night of the soul."

Dark Night of the Soul

The dark night of the soul is a time of trial, pain, solitude, and aridity. It is puzzling that this trial should occur after we have awakened, after we have transformed ourselves through the discipline of a life shaped by our awakening, and after we have tasted the joy of illumination. But as we reflect on the awakening and all that it implies, the dark night of the soul seems more familiar and even its timing becomes understandable.

"For the first time she saw and knew the Love in which life is bathed." That description of one person's experience also fits our own experience of awakening. The awakening is followed by a struggle to keep the new-found awareness alive and effective in our own lives. Then comes a time of perfect joy, when we can open our eyes "upon a world still natural but no longer illusory." But merely recognizing the love that envelops us is not enough. We must learn to love not out of selfish need nor for the joy that love brings, but for the intrinsic value of what we love. The dark night of the soul purges those aspects of love that are possessive or grasping. It is a time when everything seems to go wrong, when we fall into depression and entertain doubts concerning our former enlightenment. Our health may become frail and our friends forsake us. We seem to lack all intellectual and physical energy. The mystic who endures this period of doubt, pain, and isolation takes comfort in the assurance that the suffering has meaning and that beyond the dark night of the soul lies the unitive life. We, on the other hand, enter the experience of aridity and desolation with no sustaining vision. We lack the guideposts that the mystics have in something as simple as names for their experiences—experiences that we share with them. If we learned to name our own times of trial "dark night of the soul," we would gain the spirit to see them through, in anticipation of the unitive life that follows.

When we explored the concept of awakening, we did so in terms of mothering. We can use that same context to explore the dark night of the soul. Hagar's second desert experience provides us with a cogent description of what many mothers undergo when their offspring mature into young adults and strive to separate themselves from their parents. We must learn to love our children not as belonging to us but as belonging to themselves. We must let go and let be. This painful time of separation is prefigured in the separations associated with weaning and with starting school.[13] But the final separation that marks the child's entrance into full independent adulthood is a time of particular trial for the child and for the mother. Mothers see their children's pain and would love to take it on themselves. But they also recognize that they themselves could grow only insofar as they saw the pain through. As a consequence of this insight, they reluctantly avoid interfering with their children's pain of separation.

In the course of raising her children, the loving mother must allow for the possibility that her children will despise her. She must gradually disillusion them so that their idealization of her and their belief in her power and magic will disappear. Her children must finally see her as she is and come to recognize their own strengths.[14] Allowing those we most love to hate us is indeed the dark night of the soul. We enter it with fear, endure it with hope, and emerge from it with joy.

Unitive Life

Underhill, writing out of the tradition of Western mysticism, views spirituality in terms of the journey metaphor. A journey must have a goal, and Underhill asserts that the true goal of the mystic quest is the unitive life. The unitive life is characterized by an end to the previous oscillations between struggle and peace, renewed struggle and renewed peace. It brings about a state of equilibrium that is joyous with "intense certitude."[15]

The mystic model of a linear progression to a goal does not represent the only way of achieving the unitive life. Nevertheless, the five stages described by Underhill provide us with useful guideposts that allow us to make sense of experiences we may not otherwise understand. Once we accept that our struggles in daily life are the heroic struggles of the spiritual life, we can view our triumphs in the same way. We were born connected, united, at one. In the course of our development we lose the connection, we recover it, we forget it again, we rediscover it, but the basic unity continues as an underlying affirmation throughout our life.

After the pain of a trial that has been endured and triumphed over, we recover the unity that was waiting all along to be noticed. The unitive life does not insure us against pain. The surface may in fact continue to be as tempestuous as ever, but there is now a deep level of peace that cannot be shaken. The quickly glimpsed vision that recurs from earliest childhood on is at last truly absorbed and retains certainty in the face of all.

> Knowledge, sure, unattainable by reason, has been revealed to me, to my heart, and here am I obstinately trying to express that knowledge in words and by means of reason. . . . I shall still lose my temper with Ivan the coachman, I shall still embark on useless discussions and express my opinions inopportunely; there will still be the same wall between the sanctuary of my inmost soul and other people, even my wife; I shall probably go on scolding her in my anxiety and repenting of it afterwards; I shall still be as unable to understand with my reason why I pray, and I shall still go on praying—but my life now, my whole life, independently of anything that can happen to me, every minute of it is no longer meaningless as it was before, but has a positive meaning of goodness with which I have the power to invest it.[16]

Underhill's five landmarks are not reserved for the religious elite. We have seen that each stage corresponds to one of women's experiences in mothering: awakening corresponds to the "unselfing" that occurs in pregnancy and birth; purgation corresponds to the character formation that occurs in the regular practice of child care; illumination occurs when we finally are unified around a new center; the dark night of the soul is familiar from experiences of separation; and the unitive life is experienced when we recognize that spirituality is arrived at through the daily processes of living in this world.

"Reality indeed, the mystics say, is 'near and far'; far from our thoughts, but saturating and supporting our lives."[17] The closeness of reality has nothing to do with our location on any "journey." Reality is near at every point in our life. For some it is perceived in the expansive moments of love and joy; for others it lies in the strength that allows them to persist in their discipline or to withstand the deep pain of loss. We have seen that joy is as real as pain. The converse is also true: pain is as real as joy. Every occasion—wherever we are and whatever we may be experiencing—can be regarded as an occasion for insight and for apprehending reality. There is no place we must leave and no place where we must arrive. We need only to see clearly where we stand. Reality is found "in all those places where the direct and simple life of earth goes on."[18]

Chapter 10

Time

To gain a better understanding of spirituality, we must consider certain aspects of time: the passage of time, the shape of a life lived in terms of promises that span time, time's role in causality, transformation over time, and time's relationship to the eternal. Women's unique perspective on time—their participation in waiting and surrender—sheds light on this central category.

Worlds are made up of space, time, and some ordering principle. We have seen that space and time are Kantian categories of the understanding. We need them in order to be able to think about our world, but they themselves are hard to think about. And yet to understand more fully women's contribution to spirituality, we need to explore time, because of the role it plays in the journey model. Distance is a concept that is much easier to grasp than time—just think of trying to explain the two categories to a child. But time elapsed and distance traveled are really two different ways of expressing transformation.

CAUSALITY

Kant concerned himself with time in an effort to explain causality. Since a cause always precedes an effect, the two must be temporally related. Understanding the relationship between cause and effect is fundamental to our understanding of the world. Knowing that effects follow causes allows us, to a degree, to control events, make predictions, and assign responsibility. Also, the inevitability and immutability of cause and effect can lead to a sense of determinism and deadness. To step outside of time would be stepping outside the perspective of cause and effect and suddenly experiencing life not as the slow, mechanical march of events begun millennia ago, but as freedom.

The Burning Bush that confronted Moses was a miracle in time and about time. When we look at the bush, the past conditions our present: we have seen other things burn and we know how fire behaves. We watch. But the future we anticipate does not come to pass. The causality we think we understand does not apply. How can a burning bush remain unconsumed? It can happen only if the process takes place outside of time. In order for a cause to yield an effect, the two must occur in a temporal sequence. The meaning of the Burning Bush to Moses was that the past—what had always been—need not lead to an inevitable future. Slavery could end. Moses brought this vision back to the silent generations of Hebrew slaves in Egypt, thereby beginning the historical narrative in which the ordinary round of time and the people's experience of dailiness were shattered by time-outside-of-time. There is an antecedent but no consequence. From this point on the Israelites entered a tense, event-filled story encompassing return, plagues, exodus, and revelation.

In our own histories we have also experienced time-outside-of-time, and these episodes have also led to event-filled days yielding miracles and revelation. I think of one of those moments, during a conversation, of feeling really understood, really known. The sense that followed was not one of delight in the moment or gratification in the exchange. Rather it was a sense that this person belonged to my life. The feeling transcended time and formed the basis of covenant. I recall another such moment. It was 6 A.M., twenty-four hours after the birth of our first child. I lay awake in the hospital, my daughter's tiny bed next to mine. I couldn't think of events prior to the previous day because she had not existed before then and she now so completely filled my heart and mind. I couldn't think ahead to when I would be taking her home. Instead, I stared in wonder at her perfect form and felt contemporaneous with Creation. I understood, viscerally, the meaning of the biblical text, "And God saw all that God had made, and found it very good." That experience, too, formed the basis of covenant.

Covenants renew the world. What makes things old, stale, and weary is their inevitability—the sense that everything is merely more of the same, that there is nothing new under the sun. We are awakened to the world in many ways, most significantly through love. Love is deemed stronger than death because it instantly renews time. A child of our own and, later, a grandchild can renew the world for us and place us back again to the beginning when all things are made new.

Once we recognize the extent to which our emotional life is rooted in time, we become aware of how central a concept time is. Despair grows out of our sense that the past is irrevocable. Fear is based on our facing an unknown future. Only love seems to transcend all the categories of time. The spiritual person is imbued with love and therefore knows what time it is.

TIME AND COVENANT

We can also come to understand time in the context of covenant—a commitment that gives shape to time. We might say that a covenant is a promise whose full implications we don't understand, even as we realize that it will transform us as we try to live up to it. A covenant resembles a contract, except that we can't get out of it by hiring lawyers to find loopholes. It also resembles a promise, but it differs in that we cannot know what we are promising when we enter into it. Everything about covenants was certainly true for the Israelites as they entered into a covenant with God. We arrive at this greatest of covenants through our human commitments. The other three covenants that we, as spiritual beings, enter into are all related to time—time present, future, and past.

We look at God's promise to the Israelites to help us understand what is involved in covenant. We also examine our own human commitments to help us approach the concept of a covenant with God. "I will be with you" is the promise God makes to the Israelites. Covenants require engagement, being present in the situation with the other partner to the covenant. However, presence is more than simple physical proximity. Presence means openness and attentiveness. Of course, we hold people in our hearts, but feminism has taught us that that is not sufficient: we have to hold them in our arms. Rejecting dualism means that our covenantal commitment to presence requires us not simply to think and feel but to act. (The old theological debate about the relative significance of faith and works makes no sense in a feminist perspective that rejects the dualistic formulation. Faith is always enacted and works are the fruits of faith.)

The second characteristic of God's promise is abidingness. The covenant gives shape to time and endures across all time. A covenant is not a promise for a single action but a commitment for the ways in which we will live out our lives. Covenants not only shape time, they *take* time. When we think of the people to whom we are committed, we realize that we need to spend time together and even need to "waste" time with one another, although in love, no time is ever felt to be wasted.

The third characteristic of a covenantal relationship is its centrality. Some relationships endure because they consist of nothing more than a greeting card exchanged annually. That would not be a covenantal relationship: a covenant is primary and spills over into all other aspects of our lives.

No relationships are more difficult to uphold than covenants. We enter into them because we know we won't always be at our best, but we do want the best moments of our lives to shape those other times when we are tired, defensive, or unequal to our greatest insights. Covenants give us support, but all too often it seems as if they cost life, energy, and pain. We commit ourselves because that is how we shape our humanity. We need to love with all the expense of love—and love costs even when what we love is a cat or a dog. It costs even more when the object of our love is another person. We are shaped by those we love. Certainly, each of those we have loved has taken us to places we did not want to go: into realms of illness, anger, criticism, lack of understanding, and rejection. And still we persist.

The amazing flip side of this effort is that we come to value precisely what has cost us a lot—the pet we have spent many hours with is even more loved for the amount of life and time we have poured into it; the friend we have cared for becomes more precious. This expense is precisely what is meant by covenantal faithfulness. And so we discover that the expense is part of the reward.

THE FOUR COVENANTS

Our covenant with God defines our humanity. We live in this world, but we find all our activities here lifted up and explained in terms of a relationship that transcends this world. Our covenant with God is the center around which the other three covenants are formed, but it is these other—human—covenants, with the past, present, and future that prepare us for the one we enter into with God. The human covenants are time-bound, that with God expresses eternity.

Our covenant with the future includes our covenant with the next generation—our own children or those of others. Many people, of course, are deeply committed to the next generation without being parents themselves. They care about education, the environment, and the legislation that will help the world become a better place for those who follow us.

People may think that the covenant of parenthood is simple, natural, easy. But babies aren't always cute and cuddly. They can keep you up for three nights in a row, they can fuss, and you can feel totally ineffectual as you try to comfort them. And that's the easy part. They turn into adolescents and define themselves by their opposition to you. They leave you wondering what would have happened if you hadn't been mother to this daughter—would your relationship have endured beyond that fight? You would never accept such cruelty from someone who is just a friend—it would mark the end of your friendship. But that is precisely what distinguishes a covenantal relationship from an acquaintance and even from most friendships.

Our covenant with the present is frequently embodied in a life partner—one whom we love uniquely and with full commitment—although people who have no partner can also be fully committed to the present. Love must deal with all the changes in the ones we love and in ourselves. Those we love are precisely the ones who can hurt us the most. In a covenant polite behavior will not work. We have to be honest, which means that harsh words are sometimes exchanged. We know one another well so we can say exactly those things that most upset one another. There is little with the potential to give us more pain and also more joy than an honest conversation with one we love.

Our covenant with the past is embodied in concern for our parents and the people of their generation. Many of the virtues acquired in parenting find new applications as we nurture those who were once our care-givers. But even when this covenant is not primarily expressed in terms of specific people, it finds expression in our care for tradition, for the gift of those who came before, and for the world we inherited.

All these covenants show us the changes that result from being in relationship over a long period of time. We can explore this question within the context of each of our human relationships and then ask ourselves the ultimate question: What happens when the relationship is not with another person but with God?

Each covenant in time—future, present, and past—participates in the eternal covenant with God, so all of them mark out spiritual ways. We rarely focus on one covenant to the exclusion of the other two, but each one contains expansive moments that transform the self, as well as pain-filled moments that are inherent in love (it is notable in this connection that one of the first words that babies learn is "bye-bye"). We enter into deep commitments and then repeatedly suffer the pain of separation and loss. The older generation ages and dies, our children grow and leave us. Yet we know that our love can flourish only if we stop grasping and instead love with freedom and a sense of letting go.

It would not be possible to love and commit so deeply to any of our covenants were it not for our covenant with God, which incorporates all the other covenants. It lifts them up and "holds" them even when we must release them. As a result, we face our vulnerability and our absurd tendency to fall completely and everhopefully in love, and this absurdity is the deepest wisdom. Love *is* stronger than death—stronger than all our losses—and love is the way that most invitingly leads to God.

Love, as any parent will point out, is not a vague romantic word. Love requires work, daily expression, caring, nurturing—all the categories we encountered in exploring mothering. But we can see that love demands this whether the relationship is parent to child, child to parent, or intragenerational. Indeed, the love between peers differs from the love with one in an unequal relationship, but all love is an education in covenant.

In addition to covenants with parents, spouses, children, and friends, we form commitments with animals. Our remarkable capacity to care may be the attribute that most defines our being in the image of God. We care for our pets and farm animals. Such love frequently extends to nondomesticated animals, to flowers and trees, art works, buildings, and, ultimately, even to being itself. This growth in love and commitment is what lies behind the stewardship assigned in Genesis to the first humans. It begins *not* with controlling or using but with knowing and relating. To know the name of something is to know it in the deepest sense—to know its essence. So when Adam is directed to name the animals, he is really being asked to know his fellow creatures. This knowledge can lead to commitment, and out of that commitment covenant can grow. Thus Adam's first step was to experience the animals' being, just as Abraham and Sarah had to know God before they could enter into covenant. Similarly, the Children of Israel could enter into covenant at Mount Sinai only after they had first experienced God through the signs and wonders of the Exodus and through the care they received during the fifty days in the wilderness that preceded Sinai. Experience leads to love, which in turn leads to covenant. So if we are to enter into a covenant with God, our moral imperative is to be open to experience.

The relationship of experience to covenant may be seen in the distinction between the biblical story of Creation and the story at Sinai, a sort of re-creation. In the Creation account in Genesis, the world is brought into being by a series of fiats: "Let there be light," "Let there be an expanse in the midst of water," "Let the earth sprout forth vegetation," "Let the waters bring forth swarms of living creatures." But the Sinai account in Exodus, where the Israelites were entering into their covenant with God, begins not with a series of fiats but with an introduction, "I am the Lord your God who brought you out of the land of Egypt, out of the house of bondage." At the heart of the revelation at Sinai are the experiences of meeting, responding, and relating. We turn to our other covenants—with our parents, our spouses, our children—ready to genuinely encounter our partners in covenant, to know them and respond to them, and so to ready ourselves to enter truly into the spiritual way.

TIME AND WAITING

Kafka has suggested that the root of all sin is impatience. Indeed we cannot be present when we are worried about the future—we must let ripeness, not our own anxiety, determine when to look ahead. If we fail to recognize that "to everything there is a season" and instead try somehow to control, manipulate, or force our spiritual growth, we are bound to fail in our quest. We are born with a tension between the immanent and the transcendent, and patience—retaining the tension—defines our humanity. We should neither flee to the transcendent nor disregard its call. Firmly rooted in our four covenants, we hold the tension and wait.

WOMEN'S RELATIONSHIP TO TIME

In traditional Jewish law, women are exempt from commandments based on time: they are not, for example, required to pray the morning, afternoon, and evening services required daily of men. The rabbis held that because women have a special internal relationship with time, they don't need these services to mark its external passage. One can argue that women bring special gifts to our understanding of spirituality through their regular experiences at the borders of life and death: giving birth and attending to the dying. Also, their menses serves as a monthly reminder of these same borders—potential new life, potential death.

More likely, though, is that women were exempted from the demands of prayer so that they would be free to tend the children while the men prayed. Leaving aside the question of who benefits from the declaration that women have a special relationship with time, and the question of whether a relationship to time is biological or cultural, let us explore instead how "knowing what time it is" relates to our spiritual lives.

The Judaic tradition, like the monastic tradition, has rules about when males are obliged to pray. But anyone, man or woman, who is attentive to time and the needs of the present moment will not be constrained by the time-bound laws as would those who have no relationship with time. Time can be an objective fence delineating an area, but it can also be something with which we grow in relationship, allowing us to know in a way that is curious, attentive, and caring. Time, the wall, becomes Time, the door:

> We have a little sister,
> Whose breasts are not yet formed.
> What shall we do for our sister
> When she is spoken for?
> If she be a wall,
> We will build upon it a silver battlement;
> If she be a door,
> We will panel it in cedar.[1]

Time could serve either as a constricting and narrowing structure or as an entrance to the eternal *in* time. We choose not to build battlements but to construct a welcoming, sweet-smelling door. If we recall our definition of spirituality—coming into relationship with reality—we realize that anything can be in relationship with anything else, but if the relationship is to be spiritually transforming, it must be conscious, deliberate, covenantal, personal, and loving. "The chair is three feet from the table" describes a relationship, but it is neither conscious nor self-reflective, nor is it freely chosen, to say nothing of its not being covenantal, personal, loving, or transformative. The chair stays in place because of the physical laws acting on it—gravity and inertia—not out of freedom. Unlike the chair, which stands passively, we freely and actively choose to enter God's presence, and we alternately draw closer and draw back in what amounts to a cosmic dance. Such motion and change characterize all our covenantal relationships. They are governed not by any laws but by deeply felt experiences. We come closer, we withdraw, we open up, we become shy. We turn away but then turn back to see if our covenantal partner is still there. We carry God within us but are startled to find God outside ourselves and unexpectedly real, not the product of our imagination.

TIME AND TRANSFORMATION

Through the insights we gain in trying to live up to our four covenants, we come to recognize the value in process. Being a mother is not a single event but an ongoing commitment to caring. Being a lover is, again, not a one-time act but a life lived in union and communion. Our covenants shape us, but building character takes time, and the process is anything but orderly. Character being built is like bread being prepared: the dough rises only to be punched down, then to rise again and be punched down again, until it finally rises to be baked into a nourishing entity that is the original material transformed. So, also, our trust deepens and wanes, until our life is transformed into one that is centered and grounded in our covenant. When we get more curious about waiting and begin to explore what it is, then waiting becomes an abode where we can live and find God.

All transformation requires time, but time itself does not transform: it takes time for the dough to rise, but it is the interaction between the yeast, sugar, and water—not time—that makes it rise, and it is the heat from the oven that brings about the transformation of dough into bread. Similarly, time by itself, without transformation, cannot heal. As an example, we need look no further than sibling rivalry. We see sibling rivalry handed down in the Bible from generation to generation, from Cain down to Joseph's brothers. Only a genuine change of heart—a transformation of the self—can make a difference. When we enter into time-outside-of-time, as Moses did before the Burning Bush, we experience a respite, an oasis where resentment can abate and transformation can occur.

TIME AND THE ETERNAL

As we have seen, traditional Western spirituality has always taught that we should seek the eternal in contrast to the temporal. The two are seen as being at odds with one another, and the temporal has always been regarded as an illusion, a trap—mere appearance instead of reality. But we live our lives in time, and we have found that time itself can be a gate to the eternal. All our loves and commitments can be expressed in terms of one or another facet of time: our commitment to our children in terms of the future, that to our partner in terms of the present, and that to our parents in terms of the past. Each of these commitments can be a way to approach our commitment to God, the Eternal.

The dualistic contrast between the temporal and the eternal reflects the contrast between two definitions of time. For Aristotle, time is the measurement of the before and after, and it therefore is inextricably connected to change, motion, and the transitory. For Plato, time is a moving image of eternity, a representation of what is outside or beyond time. Both of these abstract concepts need to be tested against our actual experiences. Aristotle's definition, the measurement of the before and after, conforms to our experience of all time-measuring devices: the running of sand in an hourglass, the creep of the shadow across a sundial, the motion of the hands on the face of a clock, the breakdown of radioactive carbon. The focus is on process, and we measure the passage of time without addressing time itself. Plato's definition is also familiar. We have had experiences that were both inside and outside of time, when time was suddenly not a barrier but an entrance. There have been timeless moments in living our covenants, moments when for an instant or longer we understand how each of the covenants participates in the great covenant that lifts up all the instants of our lives into the timeless.

Before reciting the *Shema*, the central Hebrew prayer affirming God's oneness, worshipers gather together the four corners of their prayer shawls, hold the fringes from these corners together, and then pray. By tradition, this gathering of the four corners refers to the ingathering of all who had been exiled and dispersed to the four corners of the world. But besides representing distance, these four corners could also represent the four covenants related to time: past, present, future, and eternal. We can understand and pray about God's unity only when we have unified ourselves, when our commitments through all time can be lifted into their relationship to the central covenant with the Eternal.

In our chapter on death, we saw the distinction between linear time and cyclical time. Linear time is unidirectional, moving from the beginning to an end of time. Cyclical time focuses on the recurrence of events (every year spring returns and ripens into summer, then fades into autumn, moving on to death in winter). Teilhard de Chardin offers what he calls "spiraling time," which combines these two views. Spiraling time uses the religious calendar, which is cyclical, but still focuses on an end of days. But what we have learned by taking our own experiences seriously and by embracing the four covenants is that we are always in the end of days, just as we can always enter into the beginning. Before we took our own experiences seriously, "the beginning" referred to some historic event long before our own being, and "the end of days" referred to some unimaginable future. But once we understood that the Bible refers to our own lives and experiences, we recognize that we can always be in the beginning, all things can be made new; we discover events about which we want to say, "It was for this that all of creation came into being, this is our end of days." We do not ignore the future but neither do we demean the present or forget the past. There are real problems with futurists who have decided, somehow, that what has not yet occurred is more important than what is happening to us right now.

We need to be where we are—in the present—while realizing that this may include a present experience of the past or a present experience of and identification with the future. We can view the future only from our present perspective and knowledge, which is why the future always surprises us—that is, we do not live in a rerun. Visiting the past is fine, as is visiting the future, although there is the temptation to try controlling. But the temptation lies not in the future itself but in the anxiety and lack of wholeness in our vision. Someone who is ill or in pain can take comfort by remembering the good times or projecting to a pain-free future. The past is always part of every moment, conditioning us to respond in different ways, and the present feels very different when we can no longer imagine a future. It is not that we are predicting or controlling the future; we are simply pointing toward a resolution, just as a phrase of music points to a cadence. But substituting a sense of motion for a static present (eternal now) is crucial. Time gives us a sense of self (self is narrative, a changing form whose elements persist and remain relatively constant). So when we step outside of time, we also cease to be self-conscious.

Entering into time-outside-of-time means that we are so thoroughly engaged that we have lost any awareness of time passing. Children seem to do it effortlessly. Spiritual people trying to return to the total presence that is the natural habitat of young children learn that it has disadvantages. Children's misery is more intense because they have no repeated memory of having been miserable and then going beyond that misery. There is no perspective that the child can bring to its current sadness. We, unlike the child, can project ahead to a time when something we look forward to will take us out of our current sadness.

We can look back at previously "hopeless" situations that have been transcended. So even though spiritual people often argue against the adult view of time and advocate living truly in the present, they also feel strongly about memory and hope. In the desert the Israelites were taught to remember all that God had done for them and to hope in the coming settlement of the Promised Land, following their own deaths.

If time were strictly linear, then remembering would mean actually being back in the past, and hoping would mean being off in the future. Past and future can, however, be the enriching harmonies in a fully developed present. We need not choose either Exodus, which is the linear perspective of the journey, or the Song of Songs—the perspective of relationship—as a lens for viewing our spiritual way, nor should we apply first one way and then the other. We choose what happens when we put both lenses together at once and focus. That is why in prayer we draw together all four covenants and all four times.

UNITY OF TIME AND SELF

We do not move beyond the past into the future. Nothing of the past is ever lost. The past is no more gone or obliterated than a bad chisel stroke made by a sculptor disappears. The sculptor does not forget the wrong cut but must somehow reshape and reconfigure the whole so that the wrong cut becomes right in a new context. We must similarly reconfigure and reshape our past lives so that wrong cuts become meaningful in a newly shaped life. We unify our past and our vision of the future. At every moment, we live in all of time. Our self-integration is part of the deceptively simple concept that God is one (as distinguished from the idea that there is one God, a measure of quantity denying a plurality of gods). While we cannot fully understand how unity applies directly to God, we, in the image of God, can take it as an imperative for ourselves: we must become one. The fundamental dualisms that turn not into differences but into oppositions have to be brought together. The secular and the sacred must interpenetrate each other so that we can learn to find God within all our daily rounds. The periods of time must be unified through the four covenants. The spiritual models of the journey and the relationship should no longer be in conflict but should be drawn into one focus. Finally, male and female should not be opposed; they should be two lenses that give depth to our view of humanity.

TIME AND SURRENDER

Women have long been considered passive and feminism has taught empowerment and agency—and women have learned from both positions. For millennia, they have served as primary care-givers—for children, for aging parents, even for their spouses. This role, though often taken on unwillingly, has educated women spiritually. Also, passivity and the allied virtue of patience, whether foisted on women or not, have also educated them spiritually. Surrender to anything less than God is enslavement or idolatry, but surrender to God is our highest freedom and good. Dante wrote that our peace is in God's will. The difficulty, of course, lies in discerning God's will.

God's will is *not* what someone tells us it is. If we return to our starting point of religion being insight into experience, we realize we can find God's will by looking inward. The search for God's will in and through the experiences of our lives changes our question when faced with adversity from "Why me?" to "Where is God in this experience?" and "What am I to do with what has happened to me?" Surrender to God and acceptance do *not* lead to quietism—a potent heresy—they lead to quiet. Quietists say that what happens is, by definition, what should happen, and so live a life of stoical resignation and inaction. Quiet is having distance and perspective, avoiding frenetic activity, and allowing every situation to guide the individual toward what is needed. It requires time and active waiting to discern patterns, but then action follows.

Do we discover or create the vision that emerges from our quiet? The answer is neither: we co-create. We cannot create out of nothing, but we do contribute to the shape of our world. Returning once more to our model of relationship, let us think of surrender in love. Surrender is both active and passive—it creates and discovers, and it is certainly a joint effort. Conversation, a basic component of relationships, is talking and listening, creating, discovering, and co-creating. Women have been taught to watch and wait, and their attentive waiting is a great spiritual gift that needs to be recognized. But since women have been waiting seemingly forever, hasn't the time come to emphasize action over passivity?

Before taking spiritual action, women must appreciate the profound significance of waiting, attentiveness, hope, trust, and surrender. They must discover what they *as women* could add to everyone's spiritual understanding. The Western mystics always portrayed the soul as female, but they rarely if ever discussed with actual women what these feminine attributes felt like from the inside. The mystics even envisioned their own souls as female in relation to a male God. But women can see their souls as female and as being in the image of a female—or at least a nonmale—God. The poet John Donne used aggressive masculine images of God: "Batter my heart, three-personed God." But God is not a batterer, seducer, or aggressor. God, like the female, waits—"at the end of days," "in the fullness of time." God is not just the Creator, God is the co-creator, so there are times when we are invited to respond. God does not engage in monologue but pauses so that we can enter into dialogue. God gives us the freedom to claim our own lives and we, in imitation, try to love without agenda across the four covenants.

This same idea of waiting and surrender comes up as well when we look at the concept of sacred time. The distinction between sacred time and profane time goes back to the seven days of Creation, when the first thing God declared "holy" was the seventh day, or Sabbath. Sacred time, then, is built into the very structure of creation. We continue to distinguish between sacred time and profane time in comparing our festivals and holidays with our ordinary, day-to-day lives. As the hours pass, we formulate plans, accumulate worries, harbor anxieties, and meet frustrations. Something has to stop this endless piling up of tension—and then we enter into sacred time.

Sabbath, as it was celebrated by the Israelites, brought release, surrender, and renewal. Observing the Sabbath is analogous to un-clenching a fist: what was tight is loosened, and what was closed opens up. Sacred time regularly allows us to experience surrender, but we don't often let this recurring sensation point out our way. The term "surrender" can conjure up the image of defeat by a hostile force, so we need fresh contexts in which to think about it. Let's look at what happens when a poppy opens. The green sheath of the poppy is split along the sides. The sun warms the poppy, but an internal force is also at work. Gradually, the sheath falls aside. The poppy is uncovered but is still tightly closed, and no force can wrench it open. A gentle breeze teases its petals, but by evening it is still not completely open. Ripeness is all. To everything there is a season. Waiting.

The sheath, which serves a definite purpose at one stage in the poppy's development, must be discarded if the poppy is to flourish. We, too, wear the sheath of our socially constructed selves, and that sheath is needed for a time, but the self must burst through for us to bloom fully. The poppy opens because of the growth within and the warmth of the sun without (both immanence and transcendence). Inside ourselves are feelings of restlessness and yearning, and outside there is beauty, desire, and love. We may be afraid to lose our deformed, constricting self, afraid to lose what we take to be our identity. Yet we know from experience that when we can forget ourselves—lose sight of our self entirely—we feel most free. Finally, we discard the dull casing that once protected us and allow our tender petals to unfurl and release all the constriction. Surrender, then, is not mere acceptance, it is perfect joy.

THE PASSAGE OF TIME

Our most personal experience of the passage of time occurs through our own aging. It is here that all the categories of time—as cause, as transformer, as shaper of selves—get tested against our own experience. We can view aging as the inevitable breakdown of our system or, like Moses at the Burning Bush, step outside of determinism and experience that all can become new. Nothing needs to be inevitable about our relationship to the world or to the people with whom we come in contact. We are still open to wonder. Lives lived in faithful relationship to our covenants are shaped by those promises. Just as one who has spent years studying dance has shaped her body to walk with a graceful posture, so our years of faithfulness have shaped our own striding through life. And a life lived in open responsiveness to call and to Presence shows us that time is not an obstacle but our partner in a great cosmic dance.

Chapter 11

A New Spirituality

Before looking further ahead at the elements that constitute our new spirituality, we need to look back briefly: let us summarize women's contribution toward expanding the limited view of spirituality offered by traditional writers.

WOMEN'S CONTRIBUTION

We began by affirming the central role played by experience. Women's experience can transform spirituality only if experience itself is taken seriously. We adopted, as a definition of religion, "insight into the common experiences of humankind," because it properly emphasizes the importance of what we do and experience in our lives. It omits matters of belief, dogma, authority, structural hierarchies, and the like, which help define and describe the traditional organized religious groups and denominations but which need not be part of a new, essential definition of religion.

Starting with our experience and then reflecting on it helps us realize that every life is significant and potentially revealing of reality. We then see that spirituality, or coming into relationship with reality, is not reserved for any select group of religious elite but is available to all. Spirituality is the culmination of our natural maturation process—it is the fulfillment of humanity. For men, this process has traditionally stressed independence, while for women, it has usually taken the form of the self's coming into relationship with others. The spiritual life, as newly informed by the normal, maturational experiences of women, can now be seen to grow out of the ordinary and to be present, unrecognized, in the lives of many.

The major tasks of life have been identified as love, work, and communal life. Women bring to the concept of love the paradigmatic example of maternal love. This love, free from the cultural expectations of courtly or romantic love, is based on caring. When mother love is our model, we become aware of all we have received. In that light, we view work as our opportunity to contribute—passing on the gift we ourselves received. Communal life provides us with a chance to recognize shared values and, through this recognition, to experience unity. Love, contribution, and unity—women's interpretation of life's tasks—are three of the positive boundary situations that women contribute to a full spirituality.

The mother-child relationship serves as a starting point for women's contribution to spirituality in another way. Reflection on that relationship leads us to recognize and acknowledge our own initial dependence. Our awareness that we were nurtured and sustained throughout this period of dependence serves to lessen our fear, to mitigate the militant posturing with which we may disguise fear and, finally, to foster trust.

Mothering is a process of total caring—physical, emotional, psychological, and intellectual. In response to the demands made by the infant, the mother must de-center the self and focus on the needs of her child. She helps form the child by "holding"—a term that describes several kinds of nurturing care. She must also know when it becomes necessary and appropriate for the child's development for her to let go. Learning to value the child as belonging to itself and learning to love without possessing are major spiritual achievements. As a mother involved in helping a child learn all its first skills, she learns to focus on achievements and not on mistakes. Her knowledge of her infant can be gained only by empathetic identification. By learning to know her infant in this way, she becomes familiar with a kind of knowing that is central to spirituality.

In seeking role models for a new spirituality, we encounter women among those who have been largely "invisible" in society. We focus on Hagar, whose example offers us an important corrective to traditional spirituality's flight to the desert. The Desert Fathers reject the world and choose to live in the wilderness, with the aim of saving their souls. Hagar, by contrast, is thrust forcibly out of her normal world into the desert. Rather than rejecting the world, she uses the desert experience to gain insight and find strength to bring back to the world. Central to our understanding of Hagar is our appreciation of her role as mother. In the desert, she focuses on the needs of her unborn child and seeks the strength to support both their lives.

Leah, our second role model, shows us a way beyond jealousy and rivalry, through compassion. What she learns while bearing four sons gives her the insight to empathize with her sister Rachel. This empathy allows her to give her son's mandrakes to Rachel, offer her maid to Jacob, and raise Rachel's two sons after their mother's death. The stories of Hagar and Leah offer us role models of women who find meaning and value in this world. Women bear and mother children not to prepare them for some ethereal other world but to help them experience and live fully in this world.

Women's perspective on the world prompts us to read the traditional mystics carefully. We find that their writings sometimes contradict one another in such a way as to suggest that their concern is not so much with another world as with a fresh perception of this world. Such a fresh perception, achieved by some of the Desert Fathers through their solitary reflection, was also achieved a thousand years later by the philosopher Immanuel Kant. It recurs daily in the lives of women involved in mothering, for whom it is a mode of knowledge that is love. A world known through love is radically different from the one we know through the scientific categories of time, space, number, quantity, antecedent, and consequence.

Even with this fresh perception, we are still left with this world's problems as presented by the negative boundary situations of circumstance, conflict, suffering, guilt, and death.

Circumstance—the influences on our lives that are beyond our willful control—is experienced by women in the contexts of pregnancy and mothering. Women learn not to flee from the fear of circumstance but to experience it. The fear, if entered into fully, finally gives way to a joy that is deeply rooted in trust.

In the processes of mothering and of teaching children to deal with conflict, women have the opportunity to acquire consciously a way of being that had been followed unconsciously. They can become aware of internal conflict, of conflict between people, and of conflict with reality. They can then try to foster trust, openness, and simplicity in their children.

Suffering grows out of incompleteness, pain, and loss. Mothering gives women an opportunity to recognize that they need not be complete in themselves—they can accept dependency, recognizing the incompleteness of all that lives. Mothering also teaches women that some pain diminishes when its meaning is understood and that all things have a natural limit.

Guilt comes to light in terms of the natural guilt that occurs in an infant when it comes to recognize that the breast it attacks belongs to the same mother who gently holds it. Along with the guilt, which arises naturally, come the opportunities for resolving the guilt: first, the mother survives in spite of the infant's "attacks" and second, she accepts the infant's smiles and coos as "reparation." Through this experience of guilt and reparation, mothers come to recognize in guilt not a reason to flee this world but a need to contribute to it.

Finally, women bring to the problem of death an unusually clear perspective that grows out of their roles of mothering and of caring for the sick and dying. Rather than meeting the problem of death by rejecting the material world, women mourn their losses and seek some values that can transcend death. The values they offer—caring for humanity, caring for nature, and creating—grow out of their experiences of mothering. Caring for infants lets them see that the central images of death—separation, disintegration, and stasis—are in opposition to what mothering provides: connection, integration, movement, growth, and change.

Through women's insights we learn that negative boundary situations need not cause us to flee the world. The negative boundary conditions displayed in the life of Elisheba, who modeled for us women's insight into mourning, do not adequately describe the human condition. Circumstance is real, but so is love; we suffer, but we also experience joy; we know conflict, but we also know unity; we feel guilt, but we also benefit from contribution; and we stand at the border not only of death but of birth. The positive boundary situations of love, joy, unity, contribution, and birth, which are so conspicuously absent in traditional formulations of spirituality, represent yet another vital contribution to a new spirituality that takes into account women's experience.

Traditional spirituality offers us a model of the individual self in a solitary struggle for salvation. By contrast, women generally view the self as essentially social and look for value in relationships. Our own experience should teach us that the individual achievement of solitude—the capacity to be alone and to profit from this state—is possible only because of our *relationship* to a nurturing mother who fostered the capacity in us. It is also characteristic of women that their struggles are for the sake of this world: if loneliness is to be healed, it must result in compassion, not solitude.

The journey metaphor that dominates traditional Western spirituality conflicts with women's view of spirituality because inherent in the metaphor is the notion of a goal, a fixed destination. Women's experience in mothering places more value in the *process* than in any final goal. We can, however, recognize in the five traditional landmarks of the spiritual journey—awakening, purgation, illumination, dark night of the soul, and unitive life—experiences that women encounter repeatedly in the course of mothering, affirming again that spirituality is not restricted to the religious elite.

UNDERSTANDING RELIGIOUS STATEMENTS

Our look at spirituality began with a definition: "Religion is insight into the common experiences of humankind." Let us begin this conclusion with a quotation that complements that definition: "the most certain truths are good for nothing if we do not put them to the test ourselves."[1] Truths are wrested out of experience. Redemptive truths— those that make a significant difference—are found within our own experiences. "It only takes a moment to tell a child all the wisdom in the world, but our whole lives are not long enough to help us understand it, because our own experience is our only light."[2] We should not simply adopt a set of beliefs. We shouldn't, not because we want to question authority or insist on individualism, but because we don't understand the beliefs. When we were children, our parents could discuss within our hearing subjects that are usually reserved for adult conversation. But lacking the experiences that their words described, we could make no sense out of what they were saying. Their statements were as concealed from us as if they had been spoken in a foreign language or written in a sealed book. Only after we had had certain experiences did their words begin to acquire meaning for us. Prior to those experiences, we neither believed nor doubted the statements—we simply didn't understand them. If they served any function for us at all, it was as place markers for experiences we would someday have.

Religious statements take on their meaning in the same way that all statements do—by referring to experience. Before we can ask whether a given statement is true, it must be meaningful to *us*. As an example of how religious statements take on meaning, let us look at the statement "Blessed are those who mourn, for they shall be comforted."[3] Before we know that all statements take on meaning only in relation to real experience, we try to grasp the idea by posing factual questions: When will they be comforted? How will they be comforted? By whom will they be comforted? After we have experienced loss and become one of those who mourn, we no longer refer the statement to "them." It now refers to ourselves, and as a consequence the questions change: What does it mean to mourn? How does it feel? Do we ever finish mourning a loss?

When we lose someone close to us, we first feel numb. Slowly, as the truth of the loss seeps in, we feel greater and greater pain. Eventually, the pain diminishes, although at certain times, perhaps holidays or other special occasions, it recurs. For the most part, however, life goes on, and the pain is absent. But there is a situation even beyond the absence of pain. Mourning is a long-term process that doesn't end when everyone thinks that you have recovered. It is a creative force concerned with recovery that moves beyond pain management. If we don't hurry mourning but allow whatever changes are taking place to continue, then "Blessed are those who mourn, for they shall be comforted" ceases to be merely an article of faith and becomes a true description of our experience. The mourned one is recovered—not in the occult, mysterious sense, but here in this world that we both inhabited, and in a way that is natural and fully consistent with our experience of reality.

We come to understand religious statements in terms of our own lives, and the truth of these statements must be tested against our experience. What women contribute to traditional spirituality are *their* experiences—of living in the world as women, as sisters, as wives, and as mothers—experiences that are not taken into account in writings on traditional spirituality.

Religious statements, as we have seen earlier, are often expressed in narrative form. Just as Moses, in traditional Western religion, is looked on as the great teacher, Miriam can play that role for women. Her story illustrates many of the insights of women's spirituality.

MIRIAM'S STORY[4]

Miriam, like Moses and Aaron, was a child of Amram and Jochebed of the tribe of Levi. The Bible preserves but five references to Miriam, yet her importance to the Israelites' story shines through even this leanest of biographical sketches. First, she is called a prophet (though her teachings are not recorded). Second, she sings to the Lord following her people's safe passage across the Red Sea. Third, she and Aaron argue with Moses about the latter's wife. Fourth, she is banished from the camp when she falls ill with leprosy and, tellingly, the Children of Israel refuse to move on until she returns. Finally, she dies and is buried in Kadesh. These five references to Miriam are all that the Bible provides us, but I believe we can reconstruct Miriam's Way from this slight evidence and from what has come down to us in an oral tradition that has gone unrecognized for millennia.

At Sinai, the Children of Israel received the Torah. That same time of revelation also saw the first explicit teaching of Miriam's Way.

Mount Sinai towered above the Israelites, the shofar blared, the thunder roared, and some of the people, in terror, told Moses:

> "You speak to us, . . . and we will obey; but let not God speak to us, lest we die." . . . So the people remained at a distance, while Moses approached the thick cloud where God was.[5]

Moses left to ascend the mountain, and the revelation intended for all the people became a personal one instead. While Moses was on Mount Sinai, Aaron was collecting gold to build a golden calf. Where was Miriam? According to the story we are imagining, Miriam gave her first teaching at this decisive time.

As Moses' absence continued, the people grew restive and frightened, and the men planned for war. But the children still had to be cared for and the meals prepared. Miriam visited the women one at a time, as they cooked and stirred, rocked their children and comforted them, and she pointed out that "revelation is taking place right now as you cook and comfort, tend the fires and nurse the young."

The men, who never did experience the revelation first-hand as Moses did, were left without anything when Moses went up Mount Sinai. They had been taken out of their former role as slaves, but now Moses, who had given them their vision of freedom, had disappeared in the cloud on the mountain, and they were left without any guidance. The women, meanwhile, returned to their tents, and Miriam was telling them that in their tasks and chores they would experience revelation.

Through these tasks and chores they had created worlds—of feeding their families, of caring for their children—and these worlds sustained them. But they did not understand the meaning of either the men's panic or their own steadiness and least of all how all this was related to revelation. Only when Miriam spoke with them, one by one, did they begin to grasp that the very future of the Israelites was at stake. When Moses returned and smashed the Tablets of the Law, and three thousand were put to the sword that day, the women comforted the living, tended the orphans, and mourned, while nursing the people who suffered from plague. All the while Miriam reminded them that this was revelation. Revelation is birth and family, dailiness and death.

She taught them about covenant. It is long habits of faithfulness that preserve us. The Children of Israel had not yet developed such habits, having left Egypt only weeks earlier. Miriam showed the people that while their covenant with God was new, those they had made with their spouses, their children, and their aging parents were a vital part of their covenant with God and that these habits of faithfulness built up over a lifetime could help preserve their commitment to God.

In considering this story, we might view the women's steadfastness at Sinai as a show of indifference to the covenant and a preoccupation with material needs and so trivialize the women's role. We might even regard their stance as one of inaction in the face of terror at the impending void and scornfully contrast it with the active response of the men. But Miriam saw the women's steadiness and their attention to daily concerns as part of a covenantal faithfulness whereby each of their lesser commitments is lifted up ,to the divine covenant in which they participate. She understood that patience was a form of love and recognized the women's strength and courage in allowing the void of Moses' absence to be a void that needn't be filled. Miriam's role was to name these experiences and to empower the women to recognize and claim their own strength.

Miriam's fundamental teaching was that our daily tasks and ongoing commitments constitute one way to the Holy. Moses and Miriam both emphasized freedom. Moses taught that freedom was a goal to be achieved by living in terms of the Mosaic law. Miriam taught that freedom was a process by which the Israelites should live, trusting their own experiences. Moses and Miriam both saw freedom as growing within the structure and habits of committed lives. Moses emphasized commitments that were centered on ritual, while Miriam stressed the idiosyncratic structures of human relationships.

While worship in the Tabernacle was a major opportunity to re-create the revelation at Sinai, it had the disadvantage that the priests were keepers of the gate, that is, they alone determined who could approach the Holy. Miriam helped the others see that the real gate is within ourselves. Our lives shape and instruct us, and we have all had experiences of revelation and redemption. We can recognize the sacred text because it is present in our life stories to take, value, and remember. There was nothing Moses brought down from Sinai that the Israelites did not already know in the marrow of their bones. Miriam taught them to recognize in revelation not something new but something true. Just as God's presence could not be restricted to the Tent of Meeting, God's revelation is not restricted to the Five Books of Moses. The Five Books of Moses stand at the center of Judaism, just as the Tabernacle stood at the center of the camp, but God's Presence is everywhere. Our paths may be different, but we ultimately arrive at a similar place: we overcome old hatreds, learn to trust, transcend earlier goals, and enter into a loving relationship with God.

Miriam helped the women locate the experience of the Divine in and through every aspect of their lives. She taught them to see their lives as sacred text, as revelation. For a historical religion, the unfolding of a life over time *is* revelation, and the women had to be taught to value and explore their own experiences.

After Miriam fought with Moses, her status was gone, but strangely, that loss was a gain. Now people who came to her were no longer seeking indirect access to Moses. During her struggle with leprosy Miriam learned about vulnerability and learned what it was like to be banished from the camp for seven days. A week is a short time, but for Miriam it was long enough to view the camp, with its problems and intrigues, from a totally different perspective. She came back—but not completely. How do you regard your skin once it has begun to flake with leprosy? And how do you reengage completely with the drama of the camp when you have once lived outside its borders? Contemplating these questions confirmed for Miriam what she had always known: that we create worlds of meaning and value, and they are suspended on fragile threads of relationships. The experience of marginality gives us the space to choose once again to relate to others and to God or to reject making such commitments.

The Miriam of our story had always taught about the role of boundaries, but the leprosy incident showed her how important—and also how potentially stultifying—religious boundaries could be. She had been pushed beyond the borders of the camp, and that experience had, in her case, engendered deeper life.

After her leprosy, Miriam no longer tried to talk to Moses and Aaron. In the time that remained to her she still had to teach the Children of Israel how to die. Moses and Aaron would die on a mountaintop, but Miriam would now die in her tent surrounded by women yearning to understand this process. She had never given birth, but having attended many births and many deaths, she concluded that the two processes are the same. Her brothers, as priests, were forbidden to minister to the dying: true to their faith forged in opposition to Egypt's cult of the dead, they would have found any signs of death polluting. Miriam, however, had found her own contact with the dead intensely purifying. How much clearer her mind and heart became after she sat with the dying, held their hands, closed their eyes. Even as she herself was dying, Miriam seemed at peace—tired and uncomfortable, perhaps, but at peace.

How could she be in pain, know that death was near, and still be at peace? Because she was unworried and unafraid, and she was being comforted by the women around her, who moistened her lips and cooled her brow. Some of the women may have been angry that Moses and Aaron had not valued what their sister knew, but Miriam told them that anger would only sap their energy. She believed she had been given more than anyone could ask, and she felt gratitude. Not one of the women had felt jealous toward her or challenged her position—what position?—and they sat with her because they loved her. And what about the pain they felt because she would no longer be there? They would use it to grow, she told them, and they did.

Miriam's lids would close over a final vision of the desert—a wilderness she had come to know as being filled with love, with pain, with desire, and with Presence. She could not know what final vision the next generation would have, yet she hoped that even in the Promised Land, they could retain the vision of the open space that held everything.

Having learned from Miriam that their lives were revealed text, the women in our story were free to store up memories and tease meaning from them, just as generations of scholars would later draw meaning from every syllable of the Five Books of Moses, hoping thereby to be brought into contact with the mind of the Maker. Miriam's Way shows us that the daily events of our lives also bring us to God. If we view our lives as sacred text, we can hope to find Presence in and through the often mundane events. Our lives are ongoing revelation from God, and at any moment we can pause and come into relationship with the Holy.

A NEW SPIRITUALITY

We have seen what women can contribute to correct or complete traditional spirituality. What remains to be described are the elements that constitute our new spirituality.

Locating Holiness

As we may learn from Miriam's Way, "Where is holiness found?" is a recurring question in religious dialogue. These are some of the answers that have been put forward:

The desert: "The desert calls him: it is a place of solitude, of silence, of forgetfulness; it is a sacred spot."[6]

The place of worship: "When we pass from the busy streets into a quiet church; where a lamp burns, and a silence reigns, the same yesterday, today, and forever."[7]

All around us: "So dinner is brought in, bread and food are offered, and God, who has not been known in the narration of the Holy Scriptures, will become known in a piece of bread."[8]

Wherever we let God in: "This is the ultimate purpose: to let God in. But we can let [God] in only where we really stand, where we live a true life."[9]

How can we choose from among these and other choices that have been proposed? First we must understand the question, "Where is holiness found?" Underlying it is the assumption that we know what holiness is. And if we can give real meaning to the concept of holiness, we must have experienced it. Knowing that, we realize that the answer to the original question does not come through the analyses and statements of others. Instead, it must grow out of our own life's experiences. Finally, we begin to review those experiences and to accord them the importance and dignity that we formerly gave only to others.

Knowing

Knowing has two familiar senses: *knowing how* (to ride a bicycle, for example) and *knowing that* (Paris is the capital of France). As we become more deeply engaged in spiritual concerns, we recognize a third kind of knowing: *knowing through being.* One instance of knowing through being occurs in our awareness of ourselves. We know ourselves from the inside—from how it feels to be us, to think our thoughts, to feel our feelings, and to live our life. This knowledge through self-identity serves as a base from which further knowing through being can take place. As our sense of self expands, we may come to know those we love, not by knowing facts about them, but by identification. We have seen such knowing exemplified in the case of a mother's knowledge of her infant, but knowing through being is not restricted to mother-child relationships. It is a form of loving that we can, in principle, have for all of being. In that light, we see that the Bodhisattva's concern for a blade of grass is one with his knowledge of the blade of grass. As we come to identify with more and more of our world by knowing through being, we become more and more related to all of reality. Spirituality—coming into relationship with reality—is fostered not by studying the lives of mystics but by increasing our knowledge-through-being by living our own lives as authentically as possible.

How We Ought to Live

When we examine a mother's relationship to her infant, we find that what the infant most needs is not "to be given the correct feed at the correct time, so much as to be fed by someone who loves feeding her own baby."[10] The best nurturing that a mother can offer her child grows out of a relationship of love. The same principle applies to nurturing a spiritual life. "To love God is a way that is no way" is Saint Bernard's cryptic way of expressing that to love is to follow no list of rules, no shalts and shalt nots with which to reassure ourselves.[11] We must be open and responsive to the ongoing, changing needs of reality in just the way that the mother is open and responsive to the needs of her child. The mother's actions come from within, not from some external authority. Similarly, our own actions "must come from the depths of [our self]—not from alien sources outside [ourselves]—but from within."[12]

Love is a way of knowing and a way of being. Rules cannot tell us how to love, but certain images might prove helpful. Earlier we considered the image of the Buddha positioned with one hand touching the earth, from which he received nourishment and support, and one hand cupped, allowing all to flow in and flow out, grateful but nongrasping. As we seek more familiar images, we turn to a consideration of two bird lovers. The first keeps a bird in a cage, while the second tends an outside bird feeder. The first exemplifies possessive "love" that distorts reality—in this case, the bird's ability to fly. The second bird lover puts out seeds in the hope that a bird will make the feeding station part of its own reality. The bird's life is not distorted, and both its occasional visits to the feeder and its absences are accepted with the same love.

Finally, let us consider an image that lies close to the experience of women, the image of the mother. We realize that there can be no single image. Being the mother of a month-old baby differs from being the mother of a two-year-old. The many changing images of the mother—now nurturing, now embracing, now sharing, now separating—speak powerfully to our changing relationship with a reality that won't stay still. If we try to grasp it, we distort or damage it. We must be open to reality, allowing it to come and go in its changing forms. We cannot possess our children and keep them in a state of infant dependency without destroying them and ourselves. Rather, we enjoy them as infants and we enjoy them as toddlers, and, most important, we accept their changing states gracefully. From our image of the mother, we also learn that our primary relationship is to our creation and not to our creator. If religious language is to have any meaning for us, we must look to our own experiences, and in our experience of loving our children, we get some notion of what the concept of "God's love" entails.

The image also helps us realize what we must have received, by making us aware of what we give. So much that is essential to our being and well-being was given to us before we had the cognitive tools to understand that what we received, over and over again, was love. If we could really know that we are loved, we would no longer seek the tokens of love—power, fame, possessions—that we now desire out of our insecurity. In the process of recovering our debt to our mothers, we recover also our grandmothers and the generations of people who loved, cared, brought forth life, and nurtured it. Finally, the image of the mother suggests that true worship is not to give thanks but to do thanks—to pass on the gift.

> Thyself and thy belongings
> Are not thine own so proper as to waste
> Thyself upon thy virtues, they on thee.
> Heaven doth with us as we with torches do,
> Not light them for themselves; for if our virtues
> Did not go forth of us, 'twere all alike
> As if we had them not.[13]

Beyond Images

Beyond the image of the mother, is there anything that can aid us on the way that is not a way? For child-rearing, Winnicott concludes that "in the long run, what we need is mothers, as well as fathers, who have found out how to believe in themselves."[14] For spirituality as well, people must believe in themselves, trust their own experiences, and act from the core of their soul. We must believe that our own lives are as serious and significant as any other life. If reality is revealed through insight into the common experiences of humankind, then we can come into relationship with reality through careful attention to the events of our own lives. There is no experience we must seek and no sign we must covet. Our own lives are full and sufficient for all the insights we need.

Because our insights come from reflection on our experiences, there is no list of experiences with which to compare our own and no acceptable standard against which to measure our lives. We understand our life by living it fully and honestly. Our experience may be troubling—we may feel the presence or the absence of God. If we experience the absence of God, then we must let it be the absence and not be tempted to fill it with a false presence.[15]

Our experiences are changeable—we move rapidly from joy to fear, from sorrow to comfort—and seem to provide a shaky foundation for our relationship with reality, yet they mirror a reality that we cannot grasp without distortion nor control without estrangement. So we *have* a way, one that is determined not by a map but by the commitment of love. It will include times of aridity and times of illumination, but it is not alien to us. It is the same way women take when they become mothers. Our lives cannot be mapped; all that determines their course is the profound commitment of loving. Sometimes we see the way; at other times we see no way at all. In the course of loving we feel pain, loss, abandonment. And in the course of loving we see reality and value transforming the world.

Notes

N.B. Biblical passages from the Hebrew Scriptures (Old Testament) follow the 1962–82 translation of the Jewish Publication Society. Passages from the Greek Scriptures (New Testament) follow the Revised Standard Version as rendered in the *New Oxford Annotated Bible*.

CHAPTER 1

1. Plato, *Phaedrus*, 244–245.
2. *The Philokalia*, vol. 1, 359.
3. Plato, *Phaedrus* and *Symposium*, passim.
4. J. H. Jowett as quoted in Harry Emerson Fosdick, *The Meaning of Prayer* (New York: Associated Press, 1920), 27.
5. Ernest Becker, *The Denial of Death*, 50.
6. Ernst Cassirer, *Language and Myth*, chapter 2.
7. John S. Dunne, *The Way of All the Earth*, xii.
8. Ibid.
9. Martin Buber, *I and Thou*, 116.
10. Ibid., 11.
11. St. Diadochos of Photiki, in *Philokalia*, vol. 1, 265.
12. Buber, *I and Thou*, 87–88.

CHAPTER 2

1. Alfred Adler, *Social Interest*, 42.
2. I Tim. 4:8 as quoted by St. Maximos the Confessor in *Philokalia*, vol. 2, 108.
3. Meister Eckhart, 35.
4. A fuller discussion of these issues may be found in Carol Ochs, *Behind the Sex of God*, chapters 7 and 8.
5. D. W. Winnicott, *The Maturational Processes and the Facilitating Environment*, 29–36.
6. Kathryn Cousins, Ewert Cousins, and Richard J. Payne, *How to Read a Spiritual Book*, 25.

7. Evelyn Underhill, *Mysticism,* 167–75.
8. Matt. 18:20.
9. Matt. 18:3.

CHAPTER 3

1. Exod. 23:9.
2. D. W. Winnicott, *The Child, the Family, and the Outside World,* 10.
3. This point and the following three are based on Winnicott, *Maturational Processes,* 49.
4. Winnicott, *Maturational Processes,* 86–87.
5. St. Gregory of Sinai, in *Writings from the Philokalia,* 79.
6. Gen. 32:25–31.
7. Exod. 33:18–23.
8. Gen. 16:10–13.
9. Job 42:5.
10. Gen. 17:15–21.
11. Gen. 21:10.
12. Gen. 21:14–21.
13. Gen. 17:16, 19.
14. Gen. 22:1–13.
15. Walter Sullivan, "The Einstein Papers."
16. Gen. 29:25–28, 30.
17. Gen. 29:31–35.
18. Gen. 30:1–2.
19. Gen. 30:3.
20. Gen. 30:6, 8.
21. Gen. 30:18.
22. Gen. 30:20.
23. Gen. 30:14–16. Mandrakes are plants whose roots were thought to possess magical powers.

CHAPTER 4

1. St. Theodoros the Great Ascetic, in *Philokalia,* vol. 2, 24.
2. Evagrios the Solitary, in *Philokalia,* vol. 1, 34.
3. Eckhart, 165.
4. Ibid., 181.
5. Ibid., 236.
6. George Herbert, "The Elixir," 311.
7. Eckhart, 9.
8. Ibid., 291.
9. Ibid., 197.

10. *Philokalia,* vol. 1, 364.
11. Eckhart, 158.
12. St. Maximos the Confessor, in *Philokalia,* vol. 2, 67.
13. Eckhart, 213.
14. Winnicott, *Maturational Processes,* 40.
15. Winnicott, *The Child,* 26–27.
16. Ibid., 45.
17. Bruno Bettelheim, "Reflections: Freud and the Soul," 52.
18. Buber, *I and Thou,* 14.
19. Sigmund Freud, *Beyond the Pleasure Principle,* in *The Standard Edition of the Complete Psychological Works of Sigmund Freud,* vol. 1, 1–64, passim.
20. Plato, *Phaedrus,* passim.
21. See, for example, *Beyond the Pleasure Principle; Group Psychology;* and *Civilization and Its Discontents.*
22. Winnicott, *The Child,* 90.
23. Exod. 3:2, 5.

CHAPTER 5

1. Karl Jaspers, *Philosophy,* vol. 2, 178.
2. John S. Dunne, *The Reasons of the Heart,* 67.
3. Anthony Bloom, *Living Prayer,* 25.
4. Cf. St. Maximos the Confessor, in *Philokalia,* vol. 2, 225.
5. Martin Buber, *The Way of Man According to the Teachings of the Hasidim,* 435.
6. Stanley Keleman, *Living Your Dying,* 121.
7. Eckhart, 23.
8. Ibid., 250.
9. Buber, *Way of Man,* 430.
10. William James, "The Will to Believe," 234.
11. John Henry Newman, "The Pillar of the Cloud."
12. Baruch Spinoza, *Ethics,* Part IV, Prop. II.
13. Dunne, *Way of All the Earth,* 69.
14. Ibid., 54.
15. Cicely Saunders, "Dying They Live: St. Christopher's Hospice," 170–72.
16. This paragraph is based on Carol Ochs, "The Sensitive Term 'Pain'," 257–58.
17. Winnicott, *The Child,* 81.
18. Matthew Fox, *Whee! We, Wee All the Way Home,* 67.
19. Winnicott, *Maturational Processes,* 22.
20. Winnicott, *The Child,* 237.

21. Elisabeth Kübler-Ross, *On Death and Dying*, 258–59.
22. Buber, *Way of Man*, 438.
23. Luke 1:46–47.
24. Franz Kafka, *I Am a Memory Come Alive*, 225.
25. Herbert Mason, *The Death of al-Hallaj*, 30.
26. St. Maximos the Confessor, in *Philokalia*, vol. 2, 279.
27. St. Diadochos of Photiki, in *Philokalia*, vol. 1, 258.

CHAPTER 6

1. Adapted from the Agada in the Talmud as quoted in *A Treasury of Jewish Folklore*, edited by Nathan Ausubel (New York: Crown, 1948), 513–14.
2. Becker, *Denial of Death*, 70.
3. Zeno (from Diogenes Laertius), in *Philosophic Classics*, 2nd ed., edited by Walter Kaufmann (Englewood Cliffs, N.J.: Prentice-Hall, 1968), vol. 1, 467.
4. See especially Kübler-Ross, *On Death and Dying*.
5. Keleman, *Living Your Dying*, 5.
6. Underhill, *Mysticism*, 169–70.
7. Kübler-Ross, *On Death and Dying*, 140.
8. Underhill, *Mysticism*, 170.
9. Kübler-Ross, *On Death and Dying*, 265.
10. Robert J. Lifton, "The Sense of Immortality," serves as a point of departure for this discussion of symbolic immortality.
11. Dunne, *Way of All the Earth*, 59.
12. Hattie R. Rosenthal, "Psychotherapy for the Dying," 631.
13. Joanna Macy, "Pearls of Despair," 3.
14. Evelyn Underhill, *Practical Mysticism*, 4.
15. Winnicott, *The Child*, 182–83.
16. Eckhart, 152.
17. Freud, "On Narcissism," in *Standard Edition*, vol. 14, 85.
18. Paul Federn, "The Reality of the Death Instinct, Especially in Melancholia," 143.
19. Song of Songs 8:6.
20. Freud, *Beyond the Pleasure Principle*, in *Standard Edition*, vol. 18, 28.
21. Albert Camus, *The Myth of Sisyphus*, 3.
22. Freud, *Analysis Terminable and Interminable*, in *Standard Edition*, vol. 23, 217.
23. Ibid., 232.
24. Cf. Josiah Royce, "The Problem of Job," in *Religion from Tolstoy to Camus*, edited by Walter Kaufmann (New York: Harper & Row, 1961), 239–57.
25. Louis Ginzberg, *The Legends of the Jews*, vol. 3, 187.

CHAPTER 7

1. Spinoza, *Ethics,* Part IV, Prop. LXVII.
2. St. Theodoros the Great Ascetic, in *Philokalia,* vol. 2, 26.
3. Simone Weil as quoted in W. H. Auden, *A Certain World* (New York: Viking Press, 1970), 306.
4. 1 John 4:18.
5. Bloom, *Living Prayer,* 14.
6. John S. Dunne, *Time and Myth,* 20.
7. Heinrich Zimmer, *Philosophies of India,* 478–79.
8. Gen. 1:6–8.
9. *Cloud of Unknowing,* 72.
10. St. Maximos the Confessor, in *Philokalia,* vol. 2, 225.
11. Spinoza, *Ethics,* Part III, Definitions of the Emotions VI and II.
12. Ibid., Part V, Prop. XXXVI.
13. Buber, *I and Thou,* 116.
14. Rabindranath Tagore, *A Tagore Reader,* 315.
15. Eckhart, 188.
16. Winnicott, *The Child,* 19–20.
17. Heraclitus, in *Philosophic Classics,* 2nd. ed., edited by Walter Kaufmann (Englewood Cliffs, N.J.: Prentice-Hall, 1968), vol. 1, 15.
18. Bettelheim, "Reflections," 52.
19. Buddha, in *Some Sayings of the Buddha,* translated by F. L. Woodward (London: Oxford University Press, 1973), 4.
20. Spinoza, *Ethics,* Part IV, Prop. II and App. XXXI.
21. Paul Carus, *The Gospel of Buddha,* 185–89.
22. Dunne, *Way of All the Earth,* 56–57.
23. Spinoza, *On the Improvement of the Understanding,* 5.
24. St. Theodoros the Great Ascetic, in *Philokalia,* vol. 2, 18.
25. Buber, *Way of Man,* 429.
26. Eckhart, 151.
27. Buber, *I and Thou,* 25.

CHAPTER 8

1. Thomas Merton, *The Wisdom of the Desert,* 3.
2. Winnicott, *Maturational Processes,* 29–36.
3. Ibid., 30.
4. Ibid., 32.
5. Edgar Jackson, *Understanding Loneliness,* 37.
6. Lewis Thomas, *The Lives of a Cell,* 73.
7. Underhill, *Practical Mysticism,* 4.
8. Buber, *I and Thou,* 11.
9. Mason, *Death of al-Hallaj,* 34.
10. Spinoza, *Ethics,* Part IV, Prop. XVIII.
11. St. Maximos the Confessor, in *Philokalia,* vol. 2, 67.

12. Spinoza, *Ethics,* Part II, Def. III.
13. Ibid., Def. VI.
14. Thomas, *Lives of a Cell,* 73.
15. Plato, *Phaedrus,* 230d.
16. Rosemarie Harding and Vincent Harding, "Racism and Sexism in America."
17. Peter G. Van Breemen, *As Bread That Is Broken,* 86.
18. St. Theodoros the Great Ascetic, in *Philokalia,* vol. 2, 21.
19. Merton, *Sign of Jonas,* 318–37.
20. The title of this section is quoted by Buber in his *Way of Man,* 435.
21. Doris Schwerin, *Diary of a Pigeon Watcher.*

CHAPTER 9

1. See, for example, works of Jean Piaget, Lawrence Kohlberg, and Daniel J. Levinson.
2. St. Gregory of Sinai, in *Writings from the Philokalia,* 65.
3. Uwe George, *In the Deserts of This Earth,* describes the surprising life in the desert.
4. Buber, *I and Thou,* 116.
5. Plato, *Republic,* 514–517.
6. Underhill, *Mysticism,* 182.
7. Num. 7:13–17.
8. Num. 11:1.
9. Underhill, *Mysticism,* 204.
10. St. Theodoros the Great Ascetic, in *Philokalia,* vol. 2, 18.
11. Mary Douglas, *Purity and Danger,* 78.
12. Underhill, *Mysticism,* 448.
13. Cf. Søren Kierkegaard's discussion of the sacrifice of Isaac in his *Fear and Trembling,* 28–29.
14. Winnicott, *The Child,* 84.
15. Underhill, *Mysticism,* 170.
16. Leo Tolstoy, *Anna Karenina,* 852–53.
17. Underhill, *Practical Mysticism,* 116.
18. Underhill, *Mysticism,* 449–50.

CHAPTER 10

1. Song of Songs 8:8–10.

CHAPTER 11

1. Georgette Leblanc, *The Bluebird for Children,* 181.
2. Ibid.
3. Matt. 5:4.

4. This section first appeared in a somewhat different form in Carol Ochs, "Miriam's Way."

5. Exod. 20:16–19.

6. André Neher, *Moses and the Vocation of the Jewish People,* 112–13.

7. Underhill, *Practical Mysticism,* 122.

8. "Mensam igitur ponunt, panes cibosque offerunt, et Deum, quem in Scripturae sacrae expositione non cognoverant, in panis fractione cognoscunt." Quoted in Underhill, *Mysticism,* 449.

9. Buber, *Way of Man,* 441.

10. Winnicott, *The Child,* 26–27.

11. St. Bernard as quoted by Eckhart, 219.

12. Eckhart, 244.

13. William Shakespeare, *Measure for Measure,* I.i.29–34.

14. Winnicott, *The Child,* 49.

15. Bloom, *Living Prayer,* 93.

Works Cited

Adler, Alfred. *Social Interest*, translated by J. Lifton and R. Vaughan. London: Faber and Faber, 1938.

Becker, Ernest. *The Denial of Death*. New York: Macmillan, 1973.

Bettelheim, Bruno. "Reflections: Freud and the Soul." *The New Yorker*, 1 March 1982, 52ff.

Bible. *The New Oxford Annotated Bible*. 2nd ed. Edited by Herbert G. May and Bruce M. Metzger. New York: Oxford University Press, 1973.

———. *A New Translation of the Holy Scriptures According to the Masoretic Text*. 3 vols. Philadelphia: Jewish Publication Society of America, 1962–82.

Bloom, Anthony. *Living Prayer*. Springfield, Ill.: Templegate, 1966.

Buber, Martin. *I and Thou*. 2nd ed. Translated by Ronald Gregor Smith. New York: Charles Scribner's Sons, 1958.

———. *The Way of Man According to the Teachings of the Hasidim*. In *Religion from Tolstoy to Camus*, edited by Walter Kaufmann. New York: Harper & Row, 1961. Pp. 425–41.

Camus, Albert. *The Myth of Sisyphus*, translated by Justin O'Brien. New York: Vintage Books, 1959.

Carus, Paul. *The Gospel of Buddha*. Chicago: Open Court, 1894.

Cassirer, Ernst. *Language and Myth*. Translated by Susanne K. Langer. New York: Harper and Brothers, 1946.

The Cloud of Unknowing. Edited by Ira Progoff. New York: Julian Press, 1957.

Cousins, Kathryn, Ewert Cousins, and Richard J. Payne. *How to Read a Spiritual Book.* New York: Paulist Press, 1981.

Day, Dorothy. *The Long Loneliness.* New York: Harper & Row, 1952.

Douglas, Mary. *Purity and Danger.* Harmondsworth, Eng.: Penguin Books, 1970.

Dunne, John S. *The Reasons of the Heart.* New York: Macmillan, 1978.

———. *Time and Myth.* New York: Doubleday, 1973.

———. *The Way of All the Earth.* New York: Macmillan, 1972.

Eckhart, Meister. *Meister Eckhart: A Modern Translation.* Translated by Raymond B. Blakney. New York: Harper & Row, 1941.

Federn, Paul. "The Reality of the Death Instinct, Especially in Melancholia," *Psychoanalytical Review* 19 (1932).

Fox, Matthew. *Whee! We, Wee All the Way Home.* Santa Fe, N.M.: Bear, 1981.

Freud, Sigmund. *The Standard Edition of the Complete Psychological Works of Sigmund Freud.* Translated under the general editorship of James Strachey. 24 vols. London: Hogarth Press, 1953–74.

George, Uwe. *In the Deserts of This Earth.* New York: Harcourt Brace Jovanovich, 1977.

Ginzberg, Louis. *The Legends of the Jews.* Philadelphia: Jewish Publication Society, 1909–38.

Harding, Rosemarie, and Vincent Harding. "Racism and Sexism in America," paper presented at the New England Regional Conference of Danforth Associates, West Lebanon, N.H., 16 October 1981.

Herbert, George. "The Elixir," in *The Country Parson* [and] *The Temple,* edited by John N. Wall Jr. New York: Paulist Press, 1981.

Jackson, Edgar. *Understanding Loneliness.* Philadelphia: Fortress Press, 1981.

James, William. "The Will to Believe," in *Religion from Tolstoy to Camus,* edited by Walter Kaufmann. New York: Harper & Row, 1961. Pp. 221–38.

Jaspers, Karl. *Philosophy,* translated by E. B. Ashton. Chicago: University of Chicago Press, 1969–71.

Kafka, Franz. *I Am a Memory Come Alive,* edited by Nahum N. Glatzer. New York: Schocken Books, 1974.

Keleman, Stanley. *Living Your Dying.* New York: Random House, 1974.

Kierkegaard, Søren. *Fear and Trembling,* edited and translated by Walter Lowrie. Princeton, N.J.: Princeton University Press, 1954.

Kübler-Ross, Elisabeth. *On Death and Dying.* New York: Macmillan, 1969.

Leblanc, Georgette. *The Bluebird for Children,* translated by Alexander Teixeira de Mattos. Boston: Silver, Burdett, 1914.

Lifton, Robert J. "The Sense of Immortality: On Death and the Continuity of Life." In *New Meanings of Death,* edited by Herman Feifel. New York: McGraw-Hill, 1977. Pp. 273–90.

Macy, Joanna. "Pearls of Despair," *Evolutionary Blues,* Summer/Fall 1981.

Mason, Herbert. *The Death of al-Hallaj: A Dramatic Narrative.* Notre Dame: University of Notre Dame Press, 1979.

Merton, Thomas. *The Sign of Jonas.* Garden City, New York: Doubleday, 1956.

———, editor and translator. *The Wisdom of the Desert: Sayings from the Desert Fathers of the Fourth Century.* New York: New Directions, 1960.

Neher, André. *Moses and the Vocation of the Jewish People.* New York: Harper & Row, 1959.

Newman, John Henry. "The Pillar of the Cloud," in *Verses on Various Occasions.* London: Burns, Oates, 1880. P. 152.

Ochs, Carol. *An Ascent to Joy.* Notre Dame: University of Notre Dame Press, 1986.

———. *Behind the Sex of God.* Boston: Beacon Press, 1977.

———. "Miriam's Way," *Cross Currents* 45 (1995): 493–509.

———. *The Noah Paradox.* Notre Dame: University of Notre Dame Press, 1991.

———. "The Sensitive Term 'Pain'," *Philosophy and Phenomenological Research* 27 (1967): 257–58.

———. *Song of the Self.* Valley Forge: Trinity Press International, 1994.

Philokalia. *The Philokalia: The Complete Text, Compiled by St. Nikodimos of the Holy Mountain and St. Makarios of Corinth.* Translated and edited by G. E. H. Palmer, P. Sherrard, and K. Ware. 4 vols. London and Boston: Faber and Faber, 1979–95.

———. *Writings from the Philokalia on Prayer of the Heart.* Edited and translated by E. Kadloubovsky and G. E. H. Palmer. London: Faber and Faber, 1951.

Plato. *The Collected Dialogues of Plato.* Edited by Edith Hamilton and Huntington Cairns. Bollingen Series 71. New York: Pantheon Books, 1961.

Rosenthal, Hattie R. "Psychotherapy for the Dying," *American Journal of Psychotherapy* 11 (1957).

Saunders, Cicely. "Dying They Live: St. Christopher's Hospice," in *New Meanings of Death,* edited by Herman Feifel. New York: McGraw-Hill, 1977. Pp. 153–79.

Schwerin, Doris. *Diary of a Pigeon Watcher.* New York: William Morrow, 1976.

Spinoza, Baruch. *Ethics, preceded by On the Improvement of the Understanding.* Edited by James Gutmann. New York: Hafner, 1955.

Sullivan, Walter. "The Einstein Papers," *New York Times,* 27–29 March 1972, 1ff.

Tagore, Rabindranath. *A Tagore Reader.* New York: Macmillan, 1961.

Thomas, Lewis. *The Lives of a Cell.* New York: Viking Press, 1974.

Tolstoy, Leo. *Anna Karenina,* edited and translated by Rosemary Edmonds. Harmondsworth, Eng.: Penguin Books, 1954.

Underhill, Evelyn. *Mysticism.* 12th ed. New York: E. P. Dutton, 1961.

———. *Practical Mysticism.* New York: E. P. Dutton, 1915.

Van Breemen, Peter G. *As Bread That Is Broken.* Denville, N.J.: Dimension Books, 1974.

Winnicott, D. W. *The Child, the Family, and the Outside World.* Harmondsworth, Eng.: Penguin Books, 1964.

————. *The Maturational Processes and the Facilitating Environment.* New York: International Universities Press, 1965.

Zimmer, Heinrich. *Philosophies of India,* edited by Joseph Campbell. Bollingen Series 26. Princeton, N.J.: Princeton University Press, 1951.

Index

Abraham, 37
acceptance, 74–75
accord, 96
adaptation, failures of, 30, 55
Adler, Alfred, 16
Allegory of the Cave, 120
aloneness, 22
Analysis Terminable and Intermin-
    able (Freud), 82–83
anchorites, 22
anger, 75
Aristotle, 138
asceticism, 19
atomism, 59–60
awakening, 75, 119–22, 126

bargaining, 75
Becker, Ernest, 7
Behind the Sex of God (Ochs), 1
Bettelheim, Bruno, 52
birth, 100–101. *See also* childbirth
Bloom, Anthony, 59
Blueland, 46
Bodhisattva, 80, 109, 155
Book of Numbers, 121
boundary situations, 57–58, 89;
    expansion of ego boundaries, 18
Buber, Martin, 3, 61–62
Buddha, 9, 76–77, 97; Parable of

the Mustard Seed, 98–99; rep-
    resentations of, 67
Buddhism, 55, 79; compassion of,
    92; eightfold path of, 47–48;
    ferryboat metaphor, 91; noble
    truths of, 47
Burning Bush, 129–30

Camus, Albert, 82
care for Being, 64
caring, 32
caring for infants, 148; knowledge
    in, 51–52
Cassirer, Ernst, 7
Catherine of Genoa, Saint, 121
Catherine of Siena, Saint, 19
causality, 129–31
Cave, Allegory of the, 120
childbirth, 100–101; Lamaze
    method, 65; psychoprophylactic
    method, 65
child care, 126–27, 147; as circum-
    stance, 62; knowledge in, 51–52,
    148
child-rearing, 147
children, 24; commitment to, 137–
    38; immortality through, 77
Christianity, 92
circumstance, 58–61, 147; fear of,
    60

173

commandments, 123
commitments: with animals, 134; to children, 137–38
communal life, 17–18
compassion, 18, 92; beyond solitude to, 103–12
compassionate understanding, 111–12
compulsion, repetition, 53–55
conception, 108
conflict, 61–62
contribution, 99–100
conversation, 141
coupling, 49
covenants, 130, 132–35; characteristics of, 131–32; with future, 132–33; with God, 132; with past, 133; with present, 133; time and, 131–32
creating, immortality through, 79–80
creation, 8, 130, 135
crowning, 66

Dante, 141
Dark night of the soul, 75, 124–25, 126–27
Day, Dorothy, 119, 121
death, 71–88; as disintegration, 80; fear of, 73; images of, 80–82; as separation, 80; as stasis, 81; women's insights into, 72–73
Deborah, 33
de Chardin, Teilhard, 138
denial, 75
depression, 75
Descartes, René, 21
desert, 154
desert experience, 104–5, 125
Desert Fathers, 20, 22, 35, 55, 146–47; categories of, 49–50; desert experience of, 104; spirituality of, 13; warning of, 115
desert journey, 117–18
despair, 130
Deuteronomy, 96
Diadochos of Photiki, Saint, 69

disintegration, death as, 80
Dunne, John S., 3, 9, 57, 99, 142; *The Way of All the Earth*, 1
dying: landmarks in, 73–76; values discovered from, 76. *See also* death

Eckhart, Meister, 3; on birth, 101; on love, 94; on otherworldliness, 55; on spirituality, 46–48; on way to God, 19, 31, 61–62
ecstasy, 5–8
ego boundaries, expansion of, 18
Einstein, Albert, 59
Elisheba, ix, 148; healing, 87–88; mourning, 83–86
Enlightenment, 9, 59–60
"Epic of Gilgamesh," 77
Eros, 54–55, 82
Esther, 33
eternal, time and, 137–40
existentialism, 71
Exodus, 27, 135, 140
experience: as challenge to journey metaphor, 118–19; role in spirituality, 11–13

failures of adaptation, 30, 55
fear, 57, 130–31; of circumstance, 60; of death, 73; entering into, 61; in mothering, 60–61
feminist spirituality, 5
ferryboat metaphor, 91
Five Books of Moses, 152, 154
flight, temptation to, 56
Francis of Assisi, Saint, 19
Freud, Sigmund: *Analysis Terminable and Interminable*, 82–83; concept of repetition compulsion, 53–55; *The Interpretation of Dreams*, 96; reinterpretation of, 52–53

Genesis, 91; Creation account, 135; Hagar's story, 34–35, 37; Leah's story, 39–42

Gilgamesh, 77
God as love, 94
guilt, 67–69, 147–48

Hagar, ix, 2, 146; desert experiences of, 104–5, 125; journey of, 116; spirituality of, 39; story of, 34–39
al-Hallaj, 68
Harding, Rosemarie, 110
healing, 86–88
hell, 117–18
Herbert, George, 46
hermits, 22, 103, 109
heroism, 33–34
Hobbes, Thomas, 72
holding, 29–30, 32, 146
holiness, 154–55
humanity, immortality through, 77–78
Hume, David, 50

"I," 63–64, 81–82
idea, definition of, 108
illumination, 75, 123–24, 126
images: of Buddha, 67; of death, 80–81; of life, 81; of mother, 156–57
immortality: symbolic, 76–80; through creating, 79–80; through humanity, 77–78; through nature, 78–79; through offspring, 77
infant care, knowledge in, 51–52, 148
inner other world, 55–56
The Interpretation of Dreams (Freud), 96
invisibles, 23–25
Isaac, 36–37
Ishmael, 36
isolate, self as, 107–8

Jacob, 34
James, William, 62
Jaspers, Karl, 57
journey: concept of, 113; desert,

117–18; to hell and back, 117–18; mountain climbing, 115–17
journey metaphor, 114–19, 125, 148; experience as challenge to, 118–19
journey to salvation, metaphor of, 23
Jowett, J. H., 7
joy, 98–99, 109
Judaism, 92, 136; traditional, 56
Judith, 33

Kafka, Franz, 68, 135
Kant, Immanuel, 48–50, 59, 129, 147
Klein, Melanie, 67
knowing, 155–56
knowing how, 155
knowing that, 155
knowing through being, 155
knowledge in infant care, 51–52, 148
Kohlberg, Lawrence, 23
Kübler–Ross, Elisabeth, 6, 68, 73–76, 119

labor pain, 65–66
Lamaze method of childbirth, 65
Leah, ix, 34, 146–47; desert experience of, 105; story of, 39–43
letting go, 30, 32
Levinson, Daniel J., 23
life: communal, 17–18; domains of, 16; how we ought to live, 156–57; images of, 81; reverence for, 16, 18
Lifton, Robert J., 6, 76
loneliness, 106–7
The Long Loneliness (Day), 119
loss, 66–67; stages of, 73
love, 16, 33, 81–83, 90–94; as context for spirituality, 19–20; defense of, 6; definition of, 92–93; as emotional experience, 13; Freudian, 53; gift of, 112; as joy, 109; mothering and, 93–94;

Platonic, 55; response to otherworldliness, 91–92; time and, 130–31; as way, 156–57

Macy, Joanna, 80
Madonna, 96
Mark the Ascetic, 49
Mary, 28, 68
Maximos the Confessor, Saint, 48, 69, 108
Merton, Thomas, 22, 111
Midrash, 30, 84
mind, categories of, 48–51
Miriam, ix; first teaching of, 151–52; story of, 150–54
mitochondria, 107, 109
moments, 48; of wholeness, 96
Moses, 34; Burning Bush and, 129–30; Five Books of Moses, 152, 154
mother (term), 3
motherhood as circumstance, 60, 62
mothering, 147; as choice of Eros versus Thanatos, 83; as context for spirituality, 2, 28–33; as contribution, 99–100; fear in, 60–61; as holding, 29–30, 146; "I" and "we" in, 64; image of, 156–57; as letting go, 30; and love, 93–94; and mystic stages, 126–27; as relationship, 111
mothering (term), 3
mountain climbing, 115–17
mourning, 83–88
Mustard Seed, Parable of the, 98–99
Mysticism (Underhill), 3
mystics, 3, 55, 141–42; contradictory nature of writings, 45–47; nature, 22
mystic stages, 23, 74, 126; and mothering, 126–27; reinterpreted, 119–22

Nahman, Rabbi, 71
nature, immortality through, 78–79

nature mystics, 22
noble truths, 47

Ochs, Carol, 1
offspring, immortality through, 77
original sin, 68–69
otherness, 20
otherworldliness, 2; inner, 55–56; love's response to, 91–92; meaning of, 47–48

pain, 64–66
pain management, 65
Parable of the Mustard Seed, 98–99
parent (term), 3
parenting (term), 3
peace, 96–97, 111–12
perception, 108
Phaedrus (Plato), 6, 109
The Philokalia, 47
place of worship, 155
Plato, 138; Allegory of the Cave, 120; *Phaedrus*, 6, 109
platonic love, 55
poverty, 59
prayer, 89–90
pregnancy, 95
provocation, 49
psalmists, 100
psychoprophylactic method of childbirth, 65
purgation, 75, 122–27

Rachel, 42
reality, 22, 127; coming into relationship with, 81
relatedness, rituals of, 123
relationship: mothering as, 111; salvation through, 107–8; value of, 110–11
religion, 5, 8–9; definition of, 1, 9, 24, 145
religious statements, 149–54
repetition compulsion, 53–55
responsibility, sense of, 105

Revelation, 8
reverence for life, 16, 18
Richard of Saint Victor, 122
rituals of relatedness, 123
role models, 33–43
Royce, Josiah, 83

Sabbath, 142
sacred time, 142
saints, 31
salvation, 103; through relationship, 107–8
Samsara, 91
Schweitzer, Albert, 16
Schwerin, Doris, 111–12
science, 50
Seasons of a Man's Life (Levinson), 23
self: de-centering, 18–19; as isolate, 107–8; killing, 18; as social, 108–11; time and, 140
self-centeredness, 12
self-consciousness, 18–19
self-sufficiency, 23
separation, 126–27; death as, 80
Shema, 138
sin, 47; original, 68–69; stages of, 49
Sinai, 135
single-pointedness, 94–95
social, self as, 108–11
Socrates, 109
solitude, 22, 105–6; to compassion from, 103–12
Song of Songs, 33, 140
soul. *See* Dark night of the soul
Spinoza, Baruch, 3; on joy, 98–99; on love, 92–93, 112; on self, 108–9
spiraling time, 138–39
spirituality, 3, 5, 9–11; context of, 15–25; definition of, 10; of Desert Fathers, 13; elements of, 154–58; experience in, 11–13; feminist, 5, 10–11; Hagar's, 39;

mothering as context for, 28–33; naturalness of, 15–16; stages or landmarks in, 23, 74, 119–22, 126; of this world, 45–56; traditional, 5, 11, 19–20, 32; walk of, 113–27; women and, 27–44; women's contribution to, x, 11, 145–49
stasis, death as, 81
statements, religious, 149–54
suffering, 63–67, 147; "I" and "we," 63–64
sufism, 80
supernatural, 78
surrender, time and, 141–43
symbolic immortality, forms of, 76–80

temptation: to flee, 56; stages of, 49
terminology, 3
Thanatos, 83
Theodoros the Great Ascetic, Saint, 99, 123
theology of Western religious systems, 20–23
Thomas, Lewis, 107, 109
time, 129–43; and covenant, 131–32; definition of, 138; and Eternal, 137–40; outside of time, 130, 139–40; passage of, 143; sacred, 142; and self, 140; spiraling, 138–39; and surrender, 141–43; and transformation, 137; and waiting, 135; women's relationship to, 135–37
Torah, 34
transcendent, 11
transformation, time and, 137
truths, noble, 47

Underhill, Evelyn, 80; on illumination, 123–24; *Mysticism*, 3; mystic stages, 23, 74–75, 119, 121, 126

unitive life, 125–27
unity, 94–97; of time and self, 140; women and, 97
unselfing, 120, 126

values discovered from dying, 76

waiting, time and, 135
walk, spiritual, 113–27
The Way of All the Earth (Dunne), 1
"we," 63–64, 81–82

Western religious systems, theology of, 20–23
wholeness, 94–96; moments of, 96
Winnicott, D. W., 3, 95, 157
women, 23–25; contribution to spirituality, x, 11, 145–49; insights into death, 72–73; reconditioned, 65–66; relationship to time, 135–37; role models, 33; and spirituality, 27–44; and unity, 97
work, 16–17
worship, place of, 155

About the Author

In addition to *Women and Spirituality* (first edition, 1983), Carol Ochs is the author of *Behind the Sex of God: Toward a New Consciousness Transcending Matriarchy and Patriarchy* (1977); *An Ascent to Joy: Transforming Deadness of Spirit* (1986); *The Noah Paradox: Time as Burden, Time as Blessing* (1991); and *Song of the Self: Biblical Spirituality and Human Holiness* (1994). She has also published many articles, in such journals as *Cross Currents, Sewanee Theological Review, Conservative Judaism,* and *Feminist Studies,* lectured widely on aspects of spirituality in synagogues, churches, and aca-demic institutions, and served as resource theologian for the Coolidge Colloquium (Cambridge, Mass., 1995, and New Haven, Conn., 1996).

Following a twenty-five-year career as professor of philosophy at Simmons College (Boston), she joined the faculty of Hebrew Union College–Jewish Institute of Religion (New York) in 1994, teaching courses in the rabbinics program on women and spirituality, desert spirituality, and spiritual direction. She was born and educated in New York City and holds a Ph.D. in philosophy from Brandeis University. She has been married since 1959 and has two grown daughters.